Mastermaths 2

Paul Briten

Head of St. Stephen's School, Twickenham

Oxford University Press

Oxford University Press, Walton Street, Oxford OX2 6DP

Oxford is a trade mark of Oxford University Press

©Paul Briten 1984 ISBN 0 19 834744 8

First published 1984
Reprinted 1985, 1988, 1989, 1990

Typeset by Tradespools Ltd, Frome; illustrated by CGS Studios, Cheltenham
Printed in Hong Kong

Contents

Contents

0 10 20 30 40 50 60 70 80 90 100 110 120 130 140 150 160 170 180 190 200

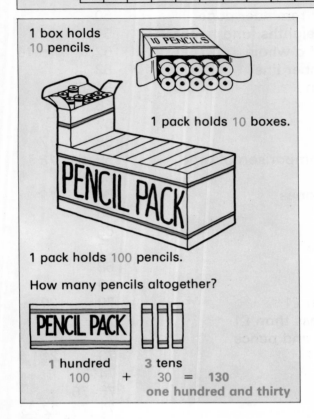

1 box holds 10 pencils.

10 PENCILS

1 pack holds 10 boxes.

PENCIL PACK

1 pack holds 100 pencils.

How many pencils altogether?

PENCIL PACK

| **1 hundred** | | **3 tens** |
| 100 | + | 30 | = | **130** |

one hundred and thirty

C Write in figures:

☆ one hundred and fifty   150

1 one hundred and sixty

2 one hundred and eighty

3 one hundred and thirty

4 one hundred and ten

5 one hundred and twenty

6 one hundred and seventy

7 one hundred and ninety

8 one hundred and forty

D Write the number that is:

☆ 16 tens   160

1 12 tens   4 11 tens   7 13 tens

2 14 tens   5 10 tens   8 19 tens

3 18 tens   6 17 tens   9 20 tens

E Write numbers for ✶'s:

☆ 100+40=✶   140

1 100+50=✶   6 100+90=✶

2 100+10=✶   7 10+30=✶

3 100+70=✶   8 100+0=✶

4 100+20=✶   9 100+80=✶

5 100+60=✶   10 100+100=✶

A Write in words:

☆ 140   one hundred and forty

1 120   5 110

2 170   6 150

3 160   7 130

4 190   8 180

B How many pencils altogether?

☆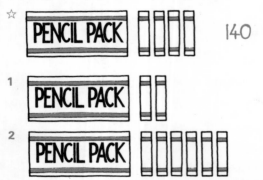

PENCIL PACK   140

1 PENCIL PACK

2 PENCIL PACK

F Copy and complete:

☆ 100 110 ✶ 130 ✶ 150 ✶ 170

100 110 120 130 140 150 160 170

1 120 ✶ 140 ✶ 160 ✶ 180

2 100 ✶ 120 130 ✶ 150 ✶ 170

3 140 ✶ 160 ✶ 180 ✶ 200

4 130 140 ✶ ✶ 170 180

5 150 160 ✶ ✶ 190 200

Place value

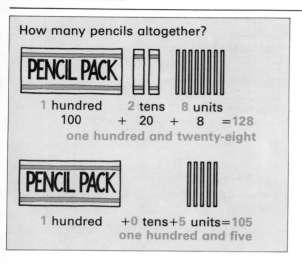

How many pencils altogether?

PENCIL PACK

1 hundred   2 tens   8 units
100   +   20   +   8   =128
one hundred and twenty-eight

PENCIL PACK

1 hundred   +0 tens+5 units=105
one hundred and five

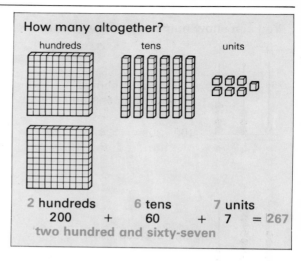

How many altogether?

hundreds   tens   units

2 hundreds   6 tens   7 units
200   +   60   +   7   = 267
two hundred and sixty-seven

Write how many pencils in 2 different ways:

☆

PENCIL PACK

147 one hundred and forty seven

1

PENCIL PACK

2

PENCIL PACK

PENCIL PACK

PENCIL PACK

PENCIL PACK

PENCIL PACK

B How many in each group?

☆
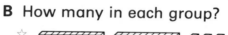
234

1

2

C Write in hundreds, tens and units:

☆ 561   5 hundreds, 6 tens, 1 unit

1   224   4   123   7   209

2   369   5   420   8   307

3   723   6   560   9   400

D Write the number that is:

☆ 3 hundreds 4 tens and 2 units   342

1   2 hundreds 1 ten and 5 units

2   7 hundreds 3 tens and 0 units

3   6 hundreds 0 tens and 9 units

4   9 hundreds 9 tens and 9 units

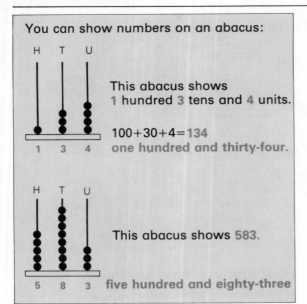

You can show numbers on an abacus:

H T U

This abacus shows
1 hundred 3 tens and 4 units.

100+30+4=134
one hundred and thirty-four.

H T U

This abacus shows 583.

five hundred and eighty-three

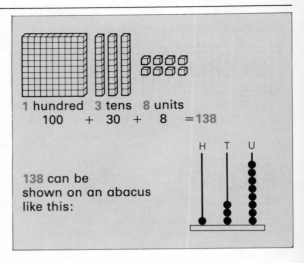

1 hundred   3 tens   8 units
    100   +   30   +   8   =138

138 can be
shown on an abacus
like this:

H T U

A Write the number shown on each
abacus in 2 different ways:

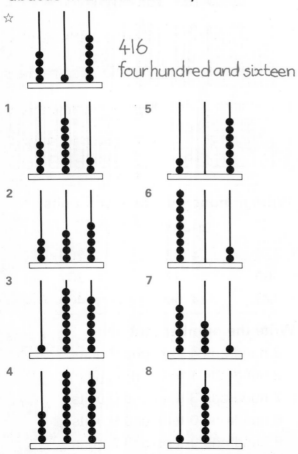

☆

416
four hundred and sixteen

1

2

3

4

5

6

7

8

B Draw an abacus picture to show
how many in each group:

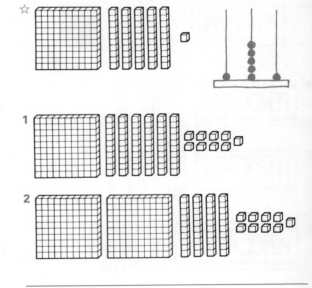

☆

1

2

C Draw abacus pictures to show
these numbers:

☆ 374

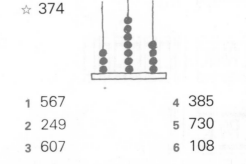

1 567   4 385

2 249   5 730

3 607   6 108

Place value

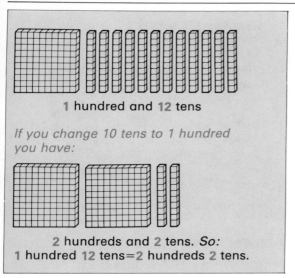

1 hundred and 12 tens

If you change 10 tens to 1 hundred you have:

2 hundreds and 2 tens. *So:*
1 hundred 12 tens=2 hundreds 2 tens.

2 hundreds and 4 tens.

If you change 1 hundred to 10 tens you have:

1 hundred 14 tens. *So:*
2 hundreds 4 tens=1 hundred 14 tens.

Use apparatus if you need to.
Change 10 tens to 1 hundred.
Write numbers for ✳'s:

☆ 1 hundreds 13 tens= 2 hundreds 3 tens

1 2 hundreds 14 tens=✳ hundreds ✳ tens

2 3 hundreds 11 tens=✳ hundreds ✳ ten

3 5 hundreds 15 tens=✳ hundreds ✳ tens

4 1 hundred 19 tens=✳ hundreds ✳ tens

5 6 hundreds 14 tens=✳ hundreds ✳ tens

C Use apparatus if you need to.
Change 1 hundred to 10 tens.
Write numbers for ✳'s:

☆ 2 hundreds 4 tens= 1 hundred 14 tens

1 4 hundreds 1 ten=✳ hundreds ✳ tens

2 6 hundreds 3 tens=✳ hundreds ✳ tens

3 3 hundreds 2 tens=✳ hundreds ✳ tens

4 2 hundreds 3 tens=✳ hundred ✳ tens

5 1 hundred 9 tens=✳ hundreds ✳ tens

Change 10 tens to 1 hundred.
Write numbers for ✳'s:

☆ 6 hundreds 18 tens= 7 hundreds 8 tens

1 3 hundreds 15 tens=✳ hundreds ✳ tens

2 7 hundreds 11 tens=✳ hundreds ✳ ten

3 8 hundreds 13 tens=✳ hundreds ✳ tens

4 1 hundred 16 tens=✳ hundreds ✳ tens

5 4 hundreds 19 tens=✳ hundreds ✳ tens

D Change 1 hundred to 10 tens.
Write numbers for ✳'s:

☆ 4 hundreds 5 tens= 3 hundreds 15 tens

1 3 hundreds 6 tens=✳ hundreds ✳ tens

2 5 hundreds 5 tens=✳ hundreds ✳ tens

3 7 hundreds 2 tens=✳ hundreds ✳ tens

4 8 hundreds 9 tens=✳ hundreds ✳ tens

5 1 hundred 0 tens=✳ hundreds ✳ tens

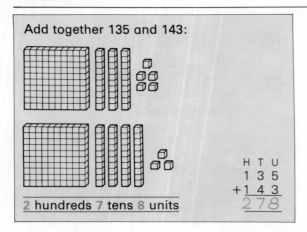

Add together 135 and 143:

2 hundreds 7 tens 8 units

```
  H T U
  1 3 5
+ 1 4 3
  2 7 8
```

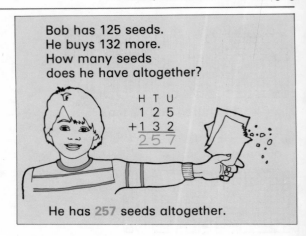

Bob has 125 seeds.
He buys 132 more.
How many seeds
does he have altogether?

```
  H T U
  1 2 5
+ 1 3 2
  2 5 7
```

He has 257 seeds altogether.

A How many altogether?

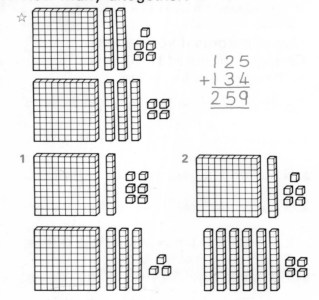

☆
```
  1 2 5
+ 1 3 4
  2 5 9
```

1

2

B Copy and complete:

☆
```
  H T U
  3 2 4
+ 1 7 5
```

```
  3 2 4
+ 1 7 5
  4 9 9
```

1
```
  H T U
  3 2 6
+ 4 1 3
```

2
```
  H T U
  1 8 7
+ 6 1 2
```

3
```
  H T U
  7 0 4
+ 1 9 3
```

4
```
  H T U
  6 3 6
+ 3 6 3
```

5
```
  H T U
  4 4 1
+ 3 5 7
```

6
```
  H T U
  6 0 6
+ 3 7 2
```

C Answer these:

☆ Tina writes 123 words and
then another 234 words.
How many words does
she write altogether?

```
  1 2 3
+ 2 3 4
  3 5 7
```

1 Fred lays 214 bricks and then 123
more. How many bricks does he lay
altogether?

2 Mr Brown plants 115 bulbs and then
another 320. How many bulbs does
he plant altogether?

3 Mary has 183 stamps. She collects
16 more. How many stamps does
she have altogether?

4 Sarah reads 2 books. One has 236
pages and the other 203 pages.
How many pages does she read
altogether?

5 A snail crawls 151 centimetres and
then another 138 centimetres.
How far does it crawl altogether?

Addition

Add together 167 and 114:

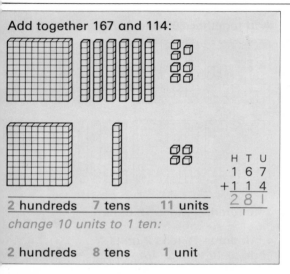

	H	T	U
	1	6	7
+	1	1	4
	2	8	1

2 hundreds   7 tens   11 units

change 10 units to 1 ten:

2 hundreds   8 tens   1 unit

Use apparatus if you need to.
Copy and complete:

```
 H T U        H T U
 2 6 5        2 6 5
+1 2 7       +1 2 7
             3 9 2
```

```
   H T U      6   H T U
   4 1 6          6 2 7
  +1 4 9         +2 6 9
```

```
   H T U      7   H T U
   5 2 9          1 1 1
  +  3 6         +8 7 9
```

```
   H T U      8   H T U
   3 7 1          2 3 8
  +4 0 9         +7 3 8
```

```
   H T U      9   H T U
   1 8 3          2 7 7
  +1 0 8         +2 1 7
```

```
   H T U     10   H T U
   1 0 8          4 8 9
  +1 0 8         +4 0 9
```

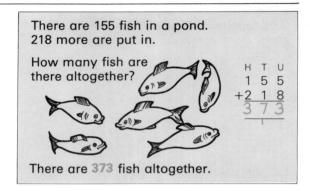

There are 155 fish in a pond.
218 more are put in.

How many fish are
there altogether?

	H	T	U
	1	5	5
+	2	1	8
	3	7	3

There are **373** fish altogether.

B Answer these:

☆ Mr Brown plants 347 flowers.
Mrs Brown plants 239 flowers.
How many flowers do
they plant altogether?

```
 H T U
 3 4 7
+2 3 9
 5 8 6
```

1 Jean writes 411 words and then
another 169 words. How many words
does she write altogether?

2 Jim eats 58 peanuts. Joe eats 133.
How many peanuts do they eat
altogether?

3 A garage sold 149 cars in 1983 and
315 cars in 1984. How many cars
were sold altogether in the 2 years?

4 There are 336 peas in each of two
packets. How many peas altogether?

C Copy and complete:

```
☆  2 3 7      2 3 7
  +1 2 8     +1 2 8
              3 6 5
```

```
1   3 4 5    3   5 3 7    5   4 2 6
   +1 2 6       +1 4 4       +2 4 6
```

```
2   3 0 7    4   2 4 6    6   7 2 3
   +1 8 6       +4 3 8       +1 0 9
```

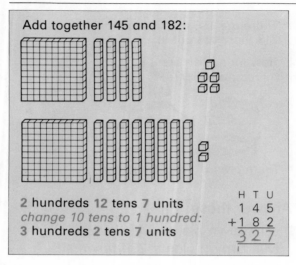

Add together 145 and 182:

2 hundreds **12** tens **7** units
change 10 tens to 1 hundred:
3 hundreds **2** tens **7** units

```
  H T U
    1 4 5
  +1 8 2
  ‾‾‾‾‾‾
    3 2 7
      ₁
```

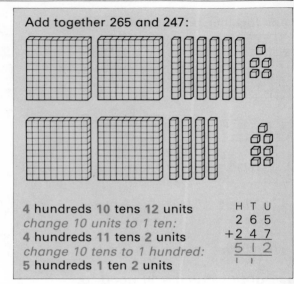

Add together 265 and 247:

4 hundreds **10** tens **12** units
change 10 units to 1 ten:
4 hundreds **11** tens **2** units
change 10 tens to 1 hundred:
5 hundreds **1** ten **2** units

```
  H T U
    2 6 5
  +2 4 7
  ‾‾‾‾‾‾
    5 1 2
    ₁ ₁
```

A Copy and complete:

☆
```
   2 7 5        2 7 5
  +3 8 2       +3 8 2
  ‾‾‾‾‾        ‾‾‾‾‾
               6 5 7
```

1
```
   5 3 9
  +2 7 0
```
4
```
   6 6 0
  +2 8 2
```
7
```
   7 7 7
  +1 7 1
```

2
```
   6 7 4
  +1 6 5
```
5
```
   3 6 2
  +2 9 3
```
8
```
   4 8 2
  +3 3 3
```

3
```
   3 8 8
  +5 5 1
```
6
```
   5 6 8
  +3 4 1
```
9
```
   5 7 0
  +2 9 9
```

B Answer these questions:

☆ A ferry carries 165 cars to France. It returns with 142 cars. How many cars are carried altogether? *307 cars*

1 A farmer milks 124 cows in the morning and 93 cows in the afternoon. How many cows does he milk altogether?

2 A baker has two ovens. He bakes 348 loaves in one oven, and 281 loaves in the other. How many loaves does he bake altogether?

3 Mrs Jenkins has £245. She collects another £274 from the bank. How much does she have altogether?

C Copy and complete:

☆
```
   1 6 2        1 6 2
  +4 5 8       +4 5 8
  ‾‾‾‾‾        ‾‾‾‾‾
               6 2 0
```

1
```
   4 3 6
  +2 8 4
```
3
```
   6 6 6
  +2 4 8
```
5
```
   4 4 5
  +2 7 7
```

2
```
   3 7 8
  +1 4 5
```
4
```
   5 2 9
  +2 9 6
```
6
```
   2 8 4
  +2 8 8
```

D Answer these:

☆ Mrs Jones eats 198 peas and then another 116 peas. How many peas does she eat altogether?
```
   1 9 8
  +1 1 6
  ‾‾‾‾‾
   3 1 4
```

1 In a chess game, Tim makes 179 moves and Tess makes 178 moves. How many moves are made altogether?

2 In Woody Avenue, there are 169 trees on one side of the road and 173 trees on the other side. How many trees altogether?

Write in words:

1	140	6	175
2	180	7	263
3	110	8	412
4	250	9	207
5	380	10	601

Write the number that is:

1	18 tens	5	10 tens
2	14 tens	6	15 tens
3	11 tens	7	19 tens
4	16 tens	8	20 tens

Write the number that is:

1 2 hundreds 3 tens and 6 units
2 6 hundreds 2 tens and 2 units
3 3 hundreds 7 tens and 0 units
4 8 hundreds 0 tens and 5 units
5 4 hundreds 4 tens and 1 unit
6 9 hundreds 3 tens and 9 units

Write the number shown on each abacus:

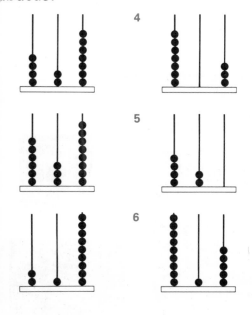

E Copy and complete:

```
1   2 6 3      4   2 7 9      7   3 9 2
   +1 2 4         +1 0 8         +1 9 9

2   6 2 8      5   3 7 5      8   8 2 7
   +  6 1         +2 8 3         +  8 9

3   4 2 6      6   4 2 4      9   5 6 3
   +1 4 5         +2 8 5         +1 6 8
```

F Answer these questions:

1 There are 183 books on one shelf and 216 books on a second shelf. How many books are there altogether?

2 An elephant eats 168 buns in the morning and 91 buns in the afternoon. How many buns does it eat altogether?

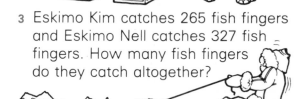

3 Eskimo Kim catches 265 fish fingers and Eskimo Nell catches 327 fish fingers. How many fish fingers do they catch altogether?

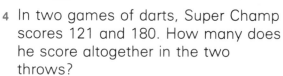

4 In two games of darts, Super Champ scores 121 and 180. How many does he score altogether in the two throws?

5 If there are 137 bean seeds in one packet and 246 bean seeds in a second packet, how many seeds are there altogether?

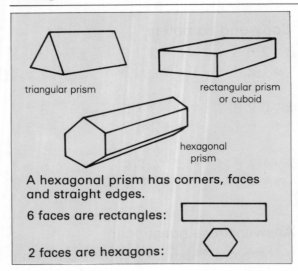

triangular prism

rectangular prism or cuboid

hexagonal prism

A hexagonal prism has corners, faces and straight edges.

6 faces are rectangles:

2 faces are hexagons:

A How many:

☆ faces on a hexagonal prism?   8

1 corners on a hexagonal prism?

2 straight edges on a hexagonal prism?

3 corners on a hexagon?

4 sides on a hexagon?

B Copy and complete:

shape	number of faces	number of corners	number of straight edges
hexagonal prism	8		
rectangular prism			
triangular prism			

C Copy and complete:

shape	number of sides	number of corners
triangle	3	
rectangle		
hexagon		

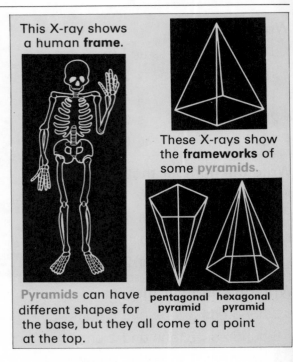

This X-ray shows a human **frame**.

These X-rays show the **frameworks** of some pyramids.

Pyramids can have different shapes for the base, but they all come to a point at the top.

pentagonal pyramid   hexagonal pyramid

D Copy and complete:

shape of base of pyramid	number of faces	number of edges	number of corners
square	5		
pentagon			
hexagon			

E Name the shape shown in each X-ray:

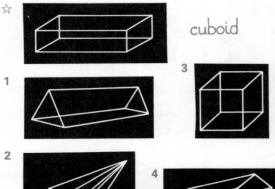

☆ cuboid

1

2

3

4

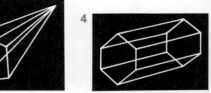

Shape

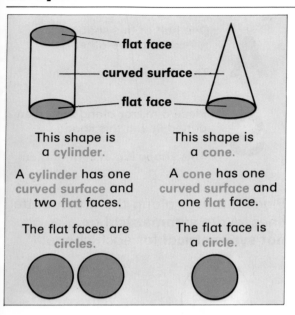

This shape is a **cylinder**.

This shape is a **cone**.

A **cylinder** has one **curved surface** and two **flat** faces.

A **cone** has one **curved surface** and one **flat** face.

The flat faces are **circles**.

The flat face is a **circle**.

What can you see in each picture, a **cone** or a **cylinder**?

cone

Write **yes** or **no**.

Can you make a cylinder using:

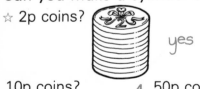

☆ 2p coins?   yes

10p coins?   4 50p coins?
20p coins?   5 1p coins?
5p coins?   6 £1 coins?

C Name three different shapes in each of these models:

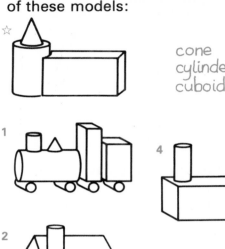

cone
cylinder
cuboid

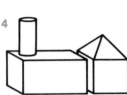

1

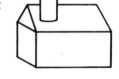

2

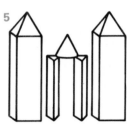

4

3

5

D Name 3 different shapes in each pattern:

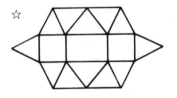

square
triangle
rectangle

1

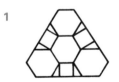

2

3

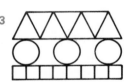

4

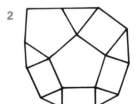

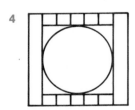

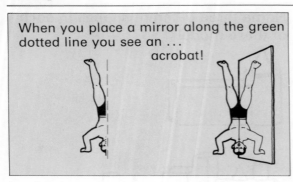

When you place a mirror along the green dotted line you see an . . .

acrobat!

One half of this shape is a **reflection** of the other half.

The shape is **symmetrical**.

Place a mirror along the green dotted line in this shape.

This shape is **not symmetrical**.

A Place a mirror along each dotted line.
What do you find in each picture?

B Place a mirror along the green dotted lines. Write **symmetrical** or **not symmetrical** for each shape:

☆ a cats head

☆ symmetrical

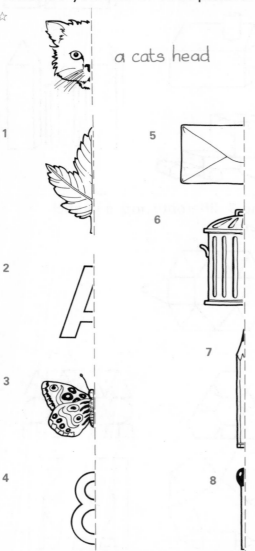

1

5

2

6

3

7

4

8

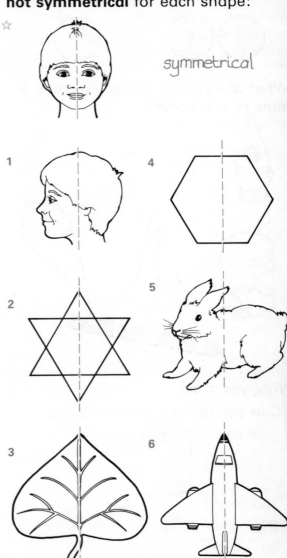

1

4

2

5

3

6

You can make **symmetrical** shapes.

Fold a piece of paper.
Cut a shape from the
folded edge.

The cut out shape
is **symmetrical**.

The fold is the
line of symmetry.

You can make shapes with
2 **lines of symmetry**.

Fold a piece of paper in half,
then in half again.

Cut a shape from the corner
as shown.

The cut out shape has
2 lines of symmetry.

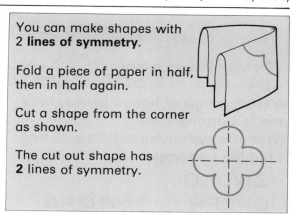

You need a mirror.
Which line is the **line of symmetry**
in each shape?
Write **green** or **black**:

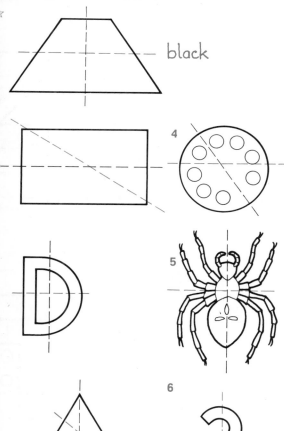

black

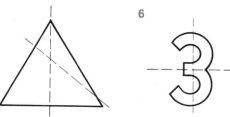

B You need a mirror.
How many of the lines shown in
each shape, are lines of symmetry?

one

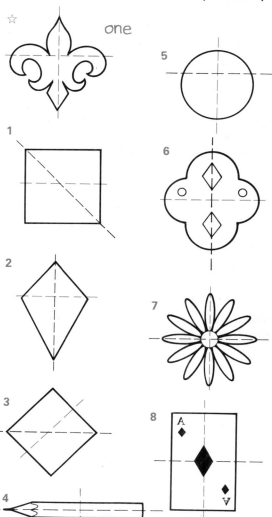

The letter **C** is symmetrical:

The letter **R** is not symmetrical.

A In each group of letters below, only one is symmetrical.
Write the symmetrical letters to find a **hidden message**:

☆ ZNDLG   D

1 OPLFR   7 VRZRG

2 JSZYL   8 EPNJR

3 FSGQO   9 LSNQA

4 NURZL   10 GFCPJ

5 QGHNS   11 PAQSR

6 JZFAQ   12 LPNTG

B Write your answer to the **hidden message**.

C Place a mirror along each **line of symmetry**.
Write the word that you find:

D Place a mirror along each **line of symmetry**.
Write the shape that you find:

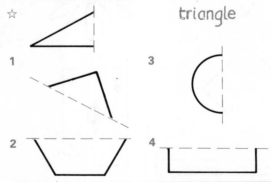

This picture shows half of a shape and the **line of symmetry**.

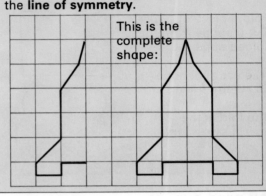

This is the complete shape:

E Copy each of these half shapes on squared paper.
Draw in the **line of symmetry**.
Complete each shape.

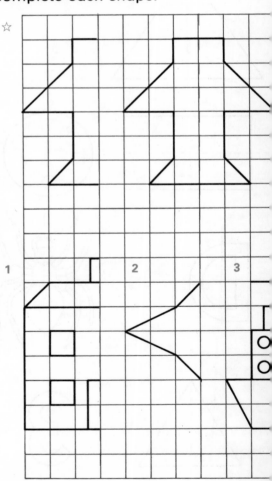

Shape

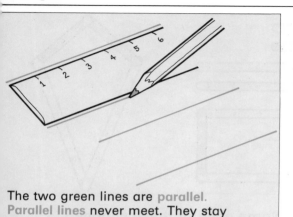

The two green lines are parallel.
Parallel lines never meet. They stay
the same distance apart.

Find two **parallel lines** in each picture:

edges of the
envelope

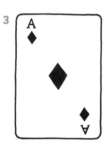

3

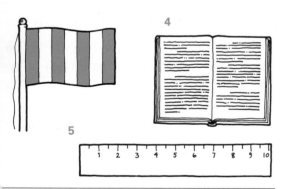

4

5

Write ten sets of **parallel lines** you
can see in your classroom:

edges of a window

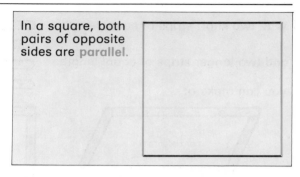

In a square, both
pairs of opposite
sides are parallel.

C Are both pairs of opposite sides
parallel in:

☆ a rectangle?   yes

1 a rhombus?   2 a parallelogram?

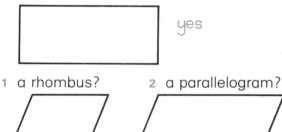

D Are all the sides the same length in:

☆ a rectangle?   no

1 a square?   3 a parallelogram?

2 a rhombus?

E Are the opposite sides the same
length in:

☆ a square?   yes

1 a parallelogram?   3 a rhombus?

2 a rectangle?

F You need a paper right angle.
How many right angles in:

☆ a square?

4

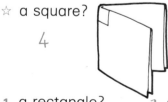

1 a rectangle?   3 a parallelogram?

2 a rhombus?

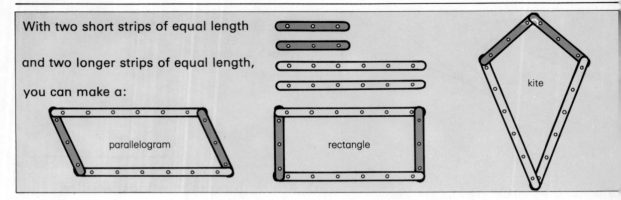

With two short strips of equal length

and two longer strips of equal length,

you can make a:

parallelogram

rectangle

kite

A Are the opposite sides the same length in:

☆ a rectangle?   yes

1 a parallelogram?   2 a kite?

B Without measuring, write the length of the green side in each shape:

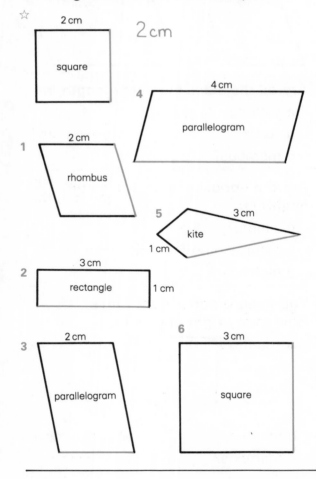

☆ 2 cm

square   2 cm

1 2 cm

rhombus

4 4 cm

parallelogram

5 3 cm

kite

1 cm

2 3 cm

rectangle   1 cm

3 2 cm

parallelogram

6 3 cm

square

C Name each of these shapes:

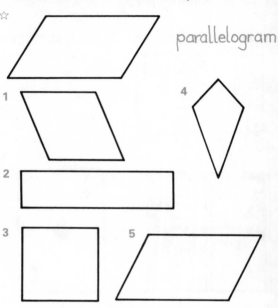

☆   parallelogram

1

2

3   5

4

D Name the shapes above that have:

☆ 4 equal sides   square, rhombus

1 both pairs of opposite sides equal in length

2 no right angles

3 both pairs of opposite sides parallel

4 no parallel sides

5 2 angles greater than a right angle

6 2 angles less than a right angle

7 no angles greater than a right angle

8 both pairs of opposite sides parallel and no right angles

Name these shapes:

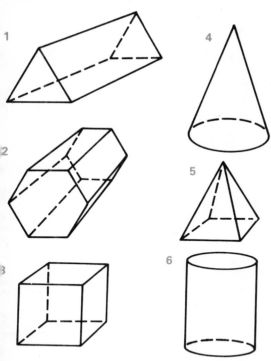

1

2

3

4

5

6

Name these shapes:

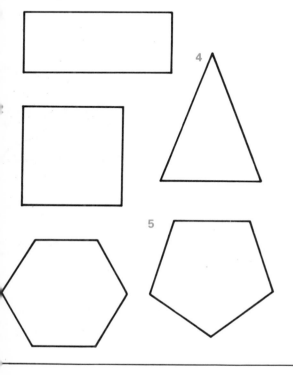

1

2

3

4

5

C In each shape below, is the dotted line a **line of symmetry**? Write **yes** or **no**:

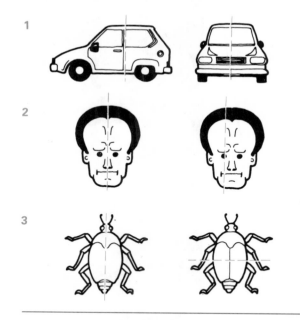

1

2

3

D Write **symmetrical** or **not symmetrical** for each letter:

1 K	5 C	9 Z
2 L	6 R	10 X
3 P	7 N	11 A
4 O	8 V	12 J

E Without measuring, write the length of the green side in each shape:

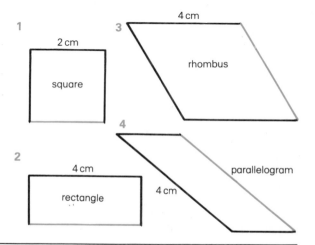

1

2 cm

square

2

4 cm

rectangle

3

4 cm

rhombus

4

4 cm

parallelogram

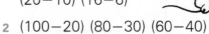

SUPER CODE MACHINE

A Work out this secret message:

☆ (16−5) (12−6) (10−6) (40−20)
   11   **6**   **4**   **20**

   w   h   a   t

1 (19−6) (16−8)

2 (60−40) (15−9) (20−6)

3 (100−20) (15−11) (16−4) (17−3)

4 (80−30) (17−12)

5 (20−2) (70−20) (13−11) (100−10)

6 (19−13) (20−6) (9−5) (20−19)

7 (90−70) (18−4) (18−14) (20−3)
   (16−10) (16−2) (100−10)

B Work out how to give your answer using only numbers.

C What is Tom saying to Jerry?

☆ (17−4)   i

1 (16−5) (18−5)
  (20−10) (16−6)

2 (100−20) (80−30) (60−40)

3 (11−5) (17−13) (18−3) (20−6)

4 (10−6)

5 (19−7) (90−40) (17−15) (17−9) (18−4

6 (9−5) (100−30) (60−10) (18−16)
  (80−60)

7 (90−70) (9−3) (17−4) (13−5)

8 (17−11) (80−30) (12−10) (19−11)
  (17−3)

Subtraction

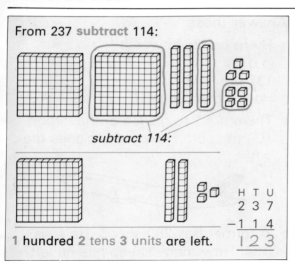

From 237 subtract 114:

subtract 114:

1 hundred 2 tens 3 units are left.

```
H T U
2 3 7
-1 1 4
1 2 3
```

Work out how many are left when you subtract **112** from each group:

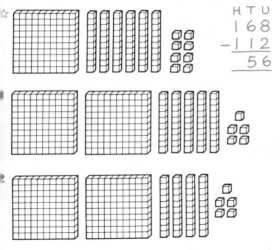

```
H T U
1 6 8
-1 1 2
  5 6
```

C Answer these:

☆ A butcher made 386 sausages.

He sold 254.
How many sausages
were left?

```
  3 8 6
-2 5 4
  1 3 2
```

1 Anna has 435 stamps. She gives away 124. How many stamps has she left?

2 Mr Jones has 359 bricks. He uses 248. How many bricks has he left?

3 There are 689 flowers in a garden. 246 are picked. How many flowers are left?

4 In a game of cricket St Mark's School scores 368 and Pen Hill School scores 224. What is the difference between the scores?

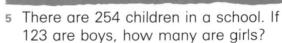

5 There are 254 children in a school. If 123 are boys, how many are girls?

6 Farmer Giles has 147 cows. Farmer Yates has 130 cows. How many more cows has Farmer Giles than Farmer Yates?

Copy and complete:

```
H T U          H T U
3 4 6          3 4 6
-2 3 2         -2 3 2
                1 1 4
```

```
H T U     3   H T U     5   H T U
4 9 7         8 4 3         2 9 9
-1 6 3        -4 1 2        -1 0 0
```

```
H T U     4   H T U     6   H T U
8 4 9         9 6 5         6 8 4
-3 1 7        -5 0 3        -1 7 3
```

D Copy and complete:

```
☆  4 7 5        4 7 5
  -1 6 4       -1 6 4
                3 1 1
```

```
1   6 6 6    3    3 4 1    5    4 5 9
   -1 2 4        -1 2 0        -2 1 0
```

```
2   8 6 8    4    6 2 7    6    3 8 6
   -3 4 6        -1 0 6        -  4 5
```

From 251 subtract 137:

You will need to change 1 ten to 10 units:

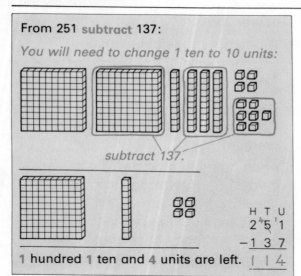

subtract 137.

```
    H  T  U
    2 ⁴5 ¹1
  - 1  3  7
```

1 hundred 1 ten and 4 units are left. | | 4

A Work out how many are left in each group when you **subtract** 118:

☆

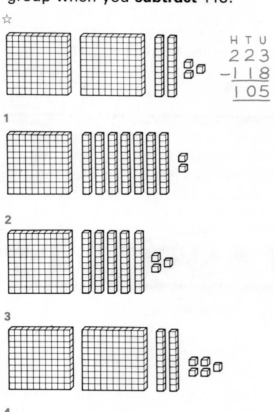

```
  H  T  U
  2  2  3
- 1  1  8
  1  0  5
```

1

2

3

4

B Answer these:

☆ There are 254 sweets in a jar. 137 are sold. How many are left?
```
   2 5 4
 - 1 3 7
   1 1 7
```

1　There are 216 planes at the airport. 109 take off. How many planes are left?

2　A farmer has 280 sheep. He sells 154. How many sheep has he left?

3　There are 724 children in a school. 309 are girls. How many are boys?

4　There are 185 pages in a book. Joe reads 106 pages. How many pages has he left to read?

5　Alan has 209 marbles. Sue has 293 marbles. How many more marbles has Sue than Alan?

6　Mr White eats 194 peas. Mrs White eats 46 peas. How many more peas does Mr White eat than Mrs White?

C Copy and complete:

```
☆   4 5 2      4 5 2
  - 2 1 5    - 2 1 5
  _____      2 3 7
```

```
1   9 6 1     4   6 6 2     7   3 6 4
  - 2 4 9       - 3 3 3       - 1 4 6
```

```
2   7 4 2     5   5 1 7     8   2 3 0
  - 2 2 6       - 1 0 9       - 1 2 1
```

```
3   4 3 2     6   7 7 3     9   8 6
  - 2 1 5       - 3 0 7       - 4 2 9
```

Subtraction

From 223 subtract 172:

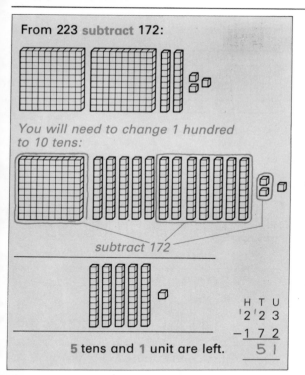

You will need to change 1 hundred to 10 tens:

subtract 172

5 tens and 1 unit are left.

$$\begin{array}{r} H\ T\ U \\ {}^1 2\ {}^1 2\ 3 \\ -1\ 7\ 2 \\ \hline 5\ 1 \end{array}$$

Work out how many are left in each group when you **subtract** 152:

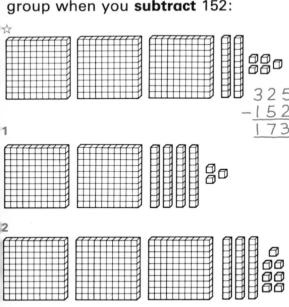

☆
$$\begin{array}{r} 325 \\ -152 \\ \hline 173 \end{array}$$

1

2

3

B Answer these:

☆ A clown has 206 custard pies. He throws 123. How many pies has he left?

$$\begin{array}{r} 206 \\ -123 \\ \hline 83 \end{array}$$

1 Jack has 263 sweets. After he has eaten 171 his tummy hurts. How many sweets has he left?

2 In a 400 metre race, Lisa has run 220 metres. How far has she left to run?

3 There are 241 people in a shop. 70 go out. How many people are left?

4 A colour television costs £309. A black and white television costs £164. What is the difference in price?

COLOUR T.V.
£309

B/W T.V.
£164

5 There are 415 children in a school. 243 are boys. How many are girls?

6 A shop has 219 loaves. 151 are sold. How many loaves are left?

C Copy and complete:

☆
$$\begin{array}{r} 506 \\ -124 \\ \hline \end{array} \qquad \begin{array}{r} 506 \\ -124 \\ \hline 382 \end{array}$$

1	$\begin{array}{r} 515 \\ -154 \end{array}$	3	$\begin{array}{r} 604 \\ -242 \end{array}$	5	$\begin{array}{r} 333 \\ -\ \ 92 \end{array}$
2	$\begin{array}{r} 926 \\ -142 \end{array}$	4	$\begin{array}{r} 283 \\ -190 \end{array}$	6	$\begin{array}{r} 515 \\ -155 \end{array}$

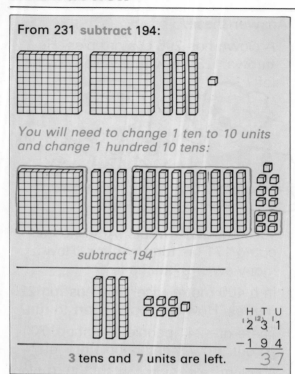

From 231 subtract 194:

You will need to change 1 ten to 10 units and change 1 hundred 10 tens:

subtract 194

3 tens and 7 units are left.

```
  H  T  U
 1 12  1
  2  3  1
 -1  9  4
    3  7
```

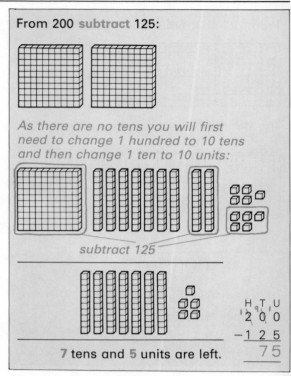

From 200 subtract 125:

As there are no tens you will first need to change 1 hundred to 10 tens and then change 1 ten to 10 units:

subtract 125

7 tens and 5 units are left.

```
  H  T  U
 1  9  1
  2  0  0
 -1  2  5
    7  5
```

A Copy and complete:

☆
```
 H T U        H T U
 2 4 2        2 4 2
-1 5 5       -1 5 5
                8 7
```

1
```
 H T U
 4 7 3
-2 9 5
```

5
```
 H T U
 3 7 5
-1 8 6
```

2
```
 H T U
 4 3 2
+2 4 5
```

6
```
 H T U
 7 7 7
-1 8 9
```

3
```
 H T U
 3 8 6
-1 9 8
```

7
```
 H T U
 5 1 4
-1 7 6
```

4
```
 H T U
 3 0 1
-1 7 5
```

8
```
 H T U
 8 2 0
-3 8 6
```

B Copy and complete:

☆
```
  3 0 0        3 0 0
 -1 2 7       -1 2 7
                1 7 3
```

1
```
  6 0 0
 -1 8 7
```

3
```
  4 0 0
 -3 4 4
```

5
```
  8 0 0
 -1 9 1
```

2
```
  3 0 0
 -1 9 6
```

4
```
  5 0 0
 -1 7 9
```

6
```
  9 0 0
 -1 7 6
```

C Use subtraction to answer these:

☆ Miss Mudd grew 324 flowers. She picked 149. How many flowers were left?
```
  3 2 4
 -1 4 5
  1 7 5
```

1 A baker bakes 400 loaves. 268 are sold. How many loaves are left?

2 There are 332 apples on a tree. 148 are picked. How many apples are left?

3 John's height is 128 centimetres. Anne's is 79 centimetres. What is the difference between their heights?

Write numbers for ✱'s:

1 12−6=✱   6 20−9=✱

2 10−4=✱   7 20−11=✱

3 16−3=✱   8 17−12=✱

4 15−8=✱   9 16−9=✱

5 19−5=✱   10 18−7=✱

Copy and complete:

1	635 −124	3	479 −128	5	756 − 39
2	392 − 72	4	632 −115	6	237 −129

Answer these questions:

1 Granny's book has 426 pages. She has read 118 pages. How many pages has she still to read?

2 A table costs £268 and 4 chairs cost £129. How much more does the table cost than the chairs?

3 There are 427 peanuts in a packet. After Trevor has eaten 109 nuts, how many are left?

4 There are 873 flowers on Joe's stall. After he sells 238 flowers, how many flowers will be left?

5 In a quiz, Bob's team scores 164 points and Carol's team scores 117 points. What is the difference between the scores?

6 Jake reads 140 pages. Sally reads 204 pages. How many more pages does Sally read than Jake?

D Copy and complete:

1	437 −263	4	729 − 86	7	600 −246
2	284 −190	5	314 −137	8	400 −181
3	621 −430	6	500 −171	9	700 −211

E Answer these questions:

1 There are 753 children in a school. If 485 are girls, how many are boys?

2 Farmer Giles' cows give 268 litres of milk. If he sells 189 litres, how much milk does he have left?

3 269 buses leave the garage. If there are 310 buses altogether, how many buses are left in the garage?

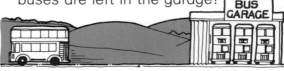

4 In a cricket match England score 431 runs and the West Indies score 520 runs. What is the difference beween the scores?

5 In one hour 500 cars pass Linda's school. If 311 pass in the first half hour, how many pass in the second half hour?

6 400 people travel to an island by ferry, and 172 people travel to the island by plane. How many more people travel by ferry?

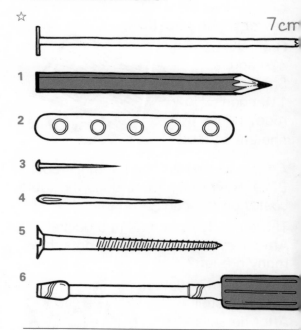

A You need a metre rule.
Are these distances longer or
shorter than 1 **metre**?

☆ the height of your classroom   longer

1 the length of your desk

2 the width of the classroom door

3 the height of your desk

4 the length of your pace

5 the width of your teacher's table

B Are these distances longer or shorter
than $\frac{1}{2}$ a **metre**?

☆ your height   longer

1 the length of your arm

2 the length of your ruler

3 your span

4 the length of your foot

5 the distance around your waist

C Would you use **metres** or
centimetres to measure these
distances?

☆ the length of your classroom   metres

1 the width of a book

2 the length of a netball court

3 the distance around your waist

4 the length of a pencil

5 the height of your school

6 the length of your foot

D Write these distances in **centimetres**:

☆ $\frac{1}{2}$ metre   50 cm

1 2 metres

2 3 metres

3 4 metres

4 5 metres

5 1$\frac{1}{2}$ metres

6 2$\frac{1}{2}$ metres

7 3$\frac{1}{2}$ metres

8 7$\frac{1}{2}$ metres

E Write the sign > or < for *'s:

☆ 97 cm * 1 m   <

1 64 cm * $\frac{1}{2}$ m

2 111 cm * 1 m

3 3 m * 400 cm

4 2 m * 250 cm

5 52 cm * $\frac{1}{2}$ m

6 300 cm * 4 m

7 2$\frac{1}{2}$ m * 249 cm

8 153 cm * 1$\frac{1}{2}$ m

F You need a ruler.
Write the length of each object to the
nearest **centimetre**:

☆   7 cm

1

2

3

4

5

6

G Write the length of each line to the
nearest **centimetre**:

☆ ——————   3 cm

1 ————————————

2 ——————————

3 ————————

4 ————————————

5 ————————

6 ————————————

Work out the total length of each
lorry and trailer: 15m + 14m = 29m

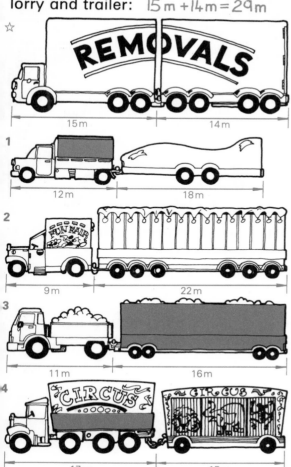

Here are the results of 2 snail races.
Work out the total distance crawled
by each snail:

snail	race 1	race 2
Creepy	18 cm	32 cm
Sleepy	16 cm	16 cm
Crawler	23 cm	41 cm
Speedy	39 cm	36 cm
Lightning	6 cm	16 cm
Jet	31 cm	19 cm
Herbert	40 cm	9 cm
Shelly	19 cm	18 cm
Super Shell	26 cm	27 cm

```
  18cm
+ 32cm
  50cm
```

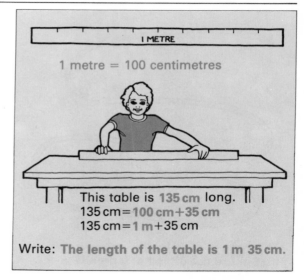

1 metre = 100 centimetres

This table is **135 cm** long.
135 cm = **100 cm + 35 cm**
135 cm = **1 m + 35 cm**

Write: **The length of the table is 1 m 35 cm.**

C Write these distances in **metres** and
centimetres:

☆ 142 cm   1m 42cm

1	176 cm	6	234 cm
2	192 cm	7	265 cm
3	109 cm	8	209 cm
4	101 cm	9	346 cm
5	160 cm	10	520 cm

D Two tables are placed end to end.
Find the total length in **metres** and
centimetres:

	length of table 1	length of table 2
☆	75 cm	93 cm
1	57 cm	68 cm
2	92 cm	49 cm
3	123 cm	124 cm
4	207 cm	99 cm
5	132 cm	149 cm
6	66 cm	166 cm
7	324 cm	147 cm
8	129 cm	129 cm
9	146 cm	99 cm
10	259 cm	51 cm

```
   75cm
+  93cm
  168cm
  1m 68cm
```

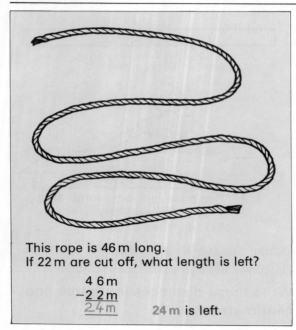

This rope is 46 m long.
If 22 m are cut off, what length is left?

```
  4 6 m
- 2 2 m
  2 4 m      24 m is left.
```

A Copy and complete:

	length of rope	length cut off	length left
☆	43 m	17 m	26m
1	33 m	12 m	*
2	46 m	18 m	*
3	32 m	27 m	*
4	40 m	21 m	*
5	80 m	52 m	*
6	63 m	36 m	*

B Copy and complete:

	length of spaghetti	length eaten	length left
☆	39 cm	25 cm	14m
1	25 cm	7 cm	*
2	30 cm	18 cm	*
3	32 cm	25 cm	*
4	39 cm	29 cm	*
5	40 cm	19 cm	*
6	24 cm	15 cm	*

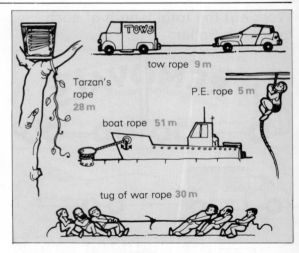

C Work out the difference in length between:

☆ the tug of war rope and the P.E. rope   25m

1 the boat rope and the tow rope
2 the P.E. rope and Tarzan's rope
3 the tow rope and the tug of war rope
4 the boat rope and Tarzan's rope
5 the P.E. rope and the boat rope
6 the tug of war rope and the boat rope

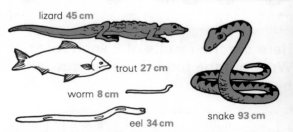

D What is the difference in length between:

☆ the lizard and the snake?   48m
1 the lizard and the worm?
2 the snake and the eel?
3 the eel and the lizard?
4 the trout and the snake?
5 the worm and the eel?
6 the lizard and the trout?

Graphs

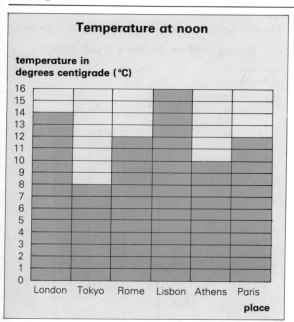

Temperature at noon

temperature in degrees centigrade (°C)

place

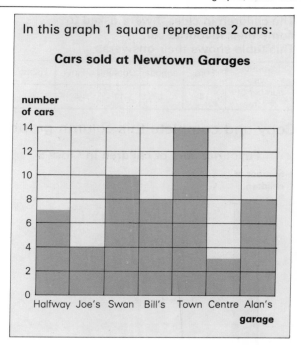

In this graph 1 square represents 2 cars:

Cars sold at Newtown Garages

number of cars

garage

Use the column graph to answer these questions. At noon:

☆ which place had the highest temperature? Lisbon

▮ which place had the lowest temperature?

2 what was the temperature in Paris?

3 what was the temperature in Rome?

4 which places had a temperature less than 11 °C?

5 which place had a temperature 4 °C higher than the temperature in Paris?

6 which 2 places had the same temperature?

▮ what was the difference in temperature between Tokyo and Lisbon?

what was the difference in temperature between London and Athens?

in which place was the temperature 2 °C lower than the temperature in Rome?

B Use the graph to answer these questions:

☆ How many cars were sold at Joe's Garage? 4

1 How many cars were sold at Alan's Garage?

2 How many cars were sold at Swan Garage?

3 How many cars were sold at Centre Garage?

4 Which 2 garages sold the same number of cars?

5 How many more cars were sold at Town Garage than at Halfway?

6 How many more cars were sold at Swan Garage than at Joe's Garage?

7 Which garage sold half as many cars as Bill's garage?

8 Which garage sold twice as many cars as Halfway?

9 How many cars were sold altogether at Newtown Garages?

The children in class 3 were asked to name their favourite car.
This table shows their answers:

favourite car	Ford	Jaguar	Datsun	Fiat	Talbot
number of children	14	1	11	4	3

A Copy and complete this column graph:

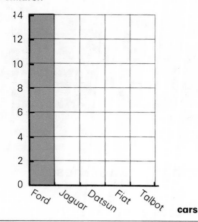

Favourite cars of children in Class 3

On this graph, 1 square represents 5 books:

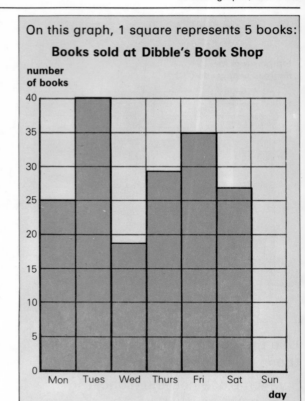

Books sold at Dibble's Book Shop

B 50 people were asked to name their favourite colour.
This table shows their answers:

favourite colour	red	blue	yellow	green	orange
number of people	8	12	10	9	11

Copy and complete this column graph:

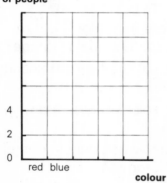

Favourite colour graph

C Use the graph to answer these questions:

☆ How many books were sold on Monday?

1 How many books were sold on Friday?

2 How many books were sold on Tuesday?

3 Try to work out from the graph the number of books sold on Thursday.

4 Try to work out from the graph the number of books sold on Saturday.

5 On which day was the shop closed?

6 How many books were sold altogether on Tuesday and Friday?

7 The shop was closed for half a day. Which day do you think this was?

8 How many more books were sold on Tuesday than on Monday?

25

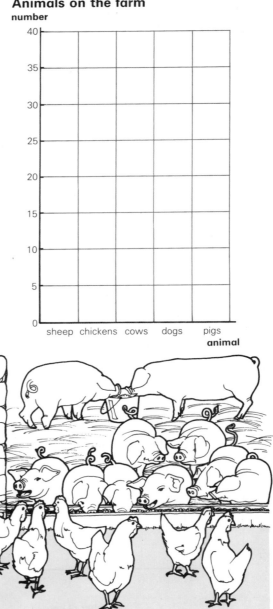

A Copy and complete this table for the farm.

animal	sheep	chickens	cows	dogs	pigs
number	35				

B Copy and complete this column graph for the farm:

Animals on the farm

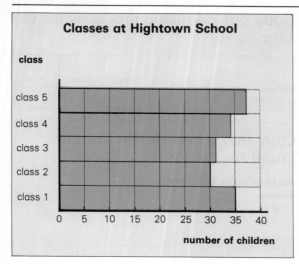

Classes at Hightown School

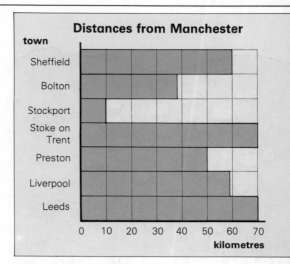

Distances from Manchester

A Use the graph above to answer these questions:

☆ Which class has the most children? class 5

1 How many children are in class 1?

2 How many children are in class 2?

3 Which class has the fewest children?

4 Try to work out how many children there are in class 3.

B 40 children were asked to name their favourite drink. This table shows their answers:

favourite drink	squash	cola	milk	tea
number of children	12	15	6	7

Copy and complete this graph:

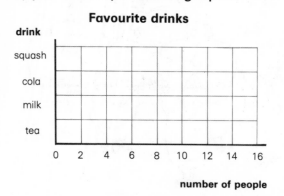

Favourite drinks

C Use the graph to answer these questions:

☆ Which town is the shortest distance from Manchester? Stockport

1 Which 2 towns are the same distance from Manchester?

2 What is the distance from Sheffield to Manchester?

3 What is the distance from Preston to Manchester?

4 Try to work out the distance from Manchester to Bolton.

D This table shows distances in kilometres from Monmouth:

town	Hereford	Newport	Ross on Wye	Abergavenny
distance from Monmouth	32 km	38 km	18 km	26 km

Copy and complete this graph:

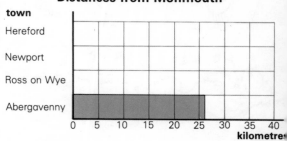

Distances from Monmouth

Burglary!

The crime: Lady Dorothy's jewels have been stolen!

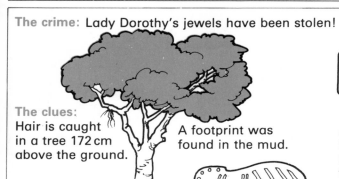

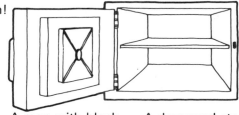

The clues:

Hair is caught in a tree 172 cm above the ground.

A footprint was found in the mud.

A man with black hair was seen running from the house.

A damaged stool with bent legs was found near the safe.

The police think:

The burglar is at least 170 cm tall.

The burglar wears size 9 shoes.

The burglar has black hair.

The burglar weighs at least 90 kg.

The information: **Pictures of suspects**

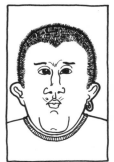
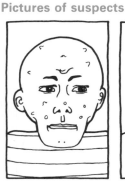

Lefty   Hutch   Pincher   Jo-Jo   Tubby

Height graph

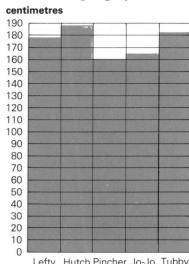

centimetres

Shoe size graph

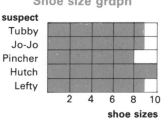

Weight graph

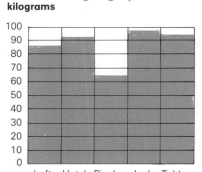

Who stole the jewels?

A Write the length of each worm to the nearest **centimetre**:

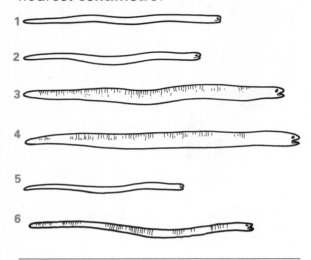

1

2

3

4

5

6

B Write these distances in **metres** and **centimetres**:

1 185 cm

2 123 cm

3 140 cm

4 208 cm

5 211 cm

6 283 cm

7 319 cm

8 405 cm

9 563 cm

10 501 cm

C Two tables are placed end to end. Write the total length in **metres** and **centimetres**:

	length of table 1	length of table 2
1	123 cm	143 cm
2	109 cm	210 cm
3	212 cm	138 cm
4	196 cm	222 cm
5	141 cm	195 cm
6	89 cm	134 cm
7	192 cm	217 cm
8	236 cm	189 cm

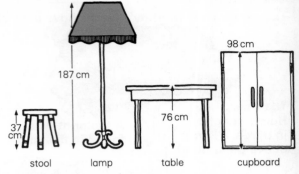

187 cm

98 cm

37 cm

76 cm

stool   lamp   table   cupboard

D Work out the difference in height between:

1 the lamp and the table

2 the cupboard and the stool

3 the table and the stool

4 the cupboard and the lamp

5 the stool and the lamp

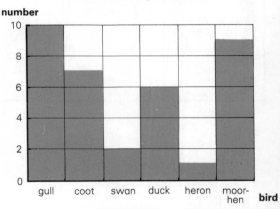

Birds seen by the lake

number

gull   coot   swan   duck   heron   moor-hen   **bird**

E Use the column graph to answer these questions:

1 How many coots were seen?

2 How many swans were seen?

3 How many herons were seen?

4 How many more gulls than ducks were seen?

5 How many more moorhens than herons were seen?

6 How many birds were seen altogether?

Hotshot

Use multiplication to find the missing numbers on these targets.
Write down the number for each ✶:

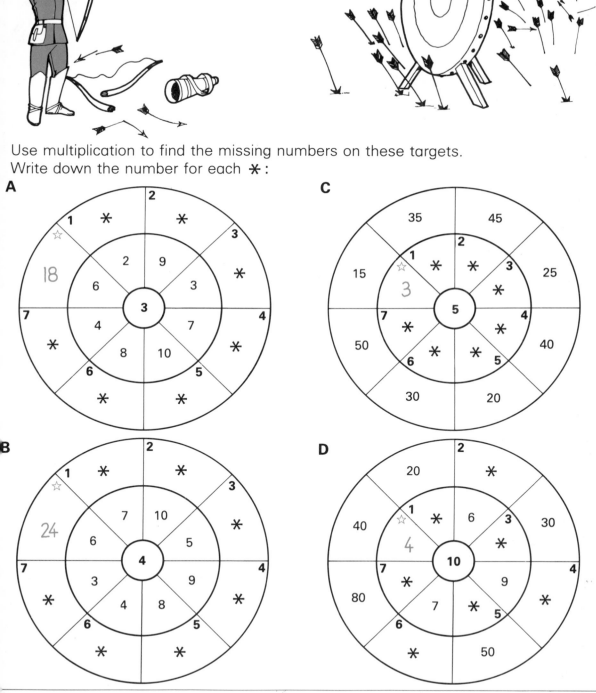

A

B

C

D

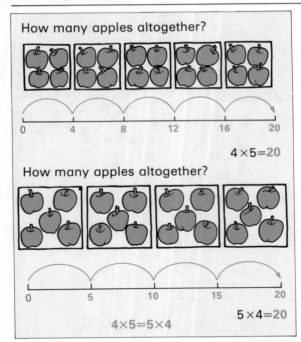

How many apples altogether?

$4 \times 5 = 20$

How many apples altogether?

$5 \times 4 = 20$

$4 \times 5 = 5 \times 4$

A Write numbers for ✳'s:

☆ $3 \times 5 = 5 \times$ ✳   3

1 $4 \times 2 = 2 \times$ ✳
2 $2 \times 10 = 10 \times$ ✳
3 $10 \times 5 = 5 \times$ ✳
4 $5 \times 3 = 3 \times$ ✳
5 $4 \times 10 = 10 \times$ ✳

6 $3 \times 2 =$ ✳ $\times 3$
7 ✳ $\times 3 = 3 \times 10$
8 $4 \times 5 =$ ✳ $\times 4$
9 $2 \times 5 =$ ✳ $\times 2$
10 $4 \times$ ✳ $= 3 \times 4$

B Find how many dots in each pattern by multiplying in 2 different ways:

☆
$2 \times 4 = 8$
$4 \times 2 = 8$

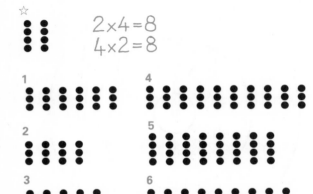

1
2
3
4
5
6

C Write numbers for ✳'s:

☆ $2 \times 6 = 12$ $6 \times 2 =$ ✳   12

1 $5 \times 4 = 20$ $4 \times 5 =$ ✳
2 $10 \times 3 = 30$ $3 \times 10 =$ ✳
3 $3 \times 5 = 15$ $5 \times 3 =$ ✳
4 $4 \times 3 = 12$ ✳ $\times 4 = 12$
5 $3 \times 8 =$ ✳ $8 \times 3 = 24$
6 $10 \times 6 = 60$ $6 \times$ ✳ $= 60$
7 ✳ $\times 9 = 45$ $9 \times 5 = 45$
8 $10 \times$ ✳ $= 90$ $9 \times 10 = 90$
9 $5 \times 7 = 35$ $7 \times$ ✳ $= 35$
10 $4 \times 8 = 32$ $8 \times 4 =$ ✳

D Write numbers for ✳'s:

☆ $2 \times 9 =$ ✳   18

1 $4 \times 5 =$ ✳
2 $6 \times 3 =$ ✳
3 $7 \times 2 =$ ✳
4 $5 \times 6 =$ ✳
5 $4 \times 8 =$ ✳
6 $3 \times 7 =$ ✳
7 $7 \times 5 =$ ✳
8 $4 \times 6 =$ ✳

9 $7 \times 4 =$ ✳
10 $9 \times 3 =$ ✳
11 $10 \times 4 =$ ✳
12 $8 \times 2 =$ ✳
13 $6 \times 4 =$ ✳
14 $9 \times 5 =$ ✳
15 $10 \times 7 =$ ✳
16 $8 \times 5 =$ ✳

E Write numbers for ✳'s:

☆ $3 \times$ ✳ $= 18$ 6

1 $2 \times$ ✳ $= 14$
2 $3 \times$ ✳ $= 21$
3 $4 \times$ ✳ $= 24$
4 $5 \times$ ✳ $= 25$
5 $10 \times$ ✳ $= 60$

6 $2 \times$ ✳ $= 18$
7 $3 \times$ ✳ $= 30$
8 $4 \times$ ✳ $= 16$
9 $5 \times$ ✳ $= 40$
10 $10 \times$ ✳ $= 100$

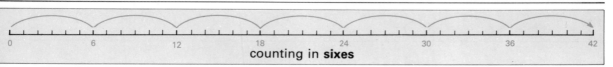

counting in **sixes**

Count in **sixes**.
Copy and complete:

☆ 6 ✳ 18 ✳ 30 ✳ 42
   6 12 18 24 30 36 42

1 12 ✳ 24 ✳ 36 ✳ 48
2 0 6 ✳ 18 ✳ 30 36
3 0 ✳ 12 ✳ 24 ✳ 36
4 6 12 ✳ ✳ 30 ✳
5 0 ✳ ✳ 18 24 ✳

You need a hundred square.
Finish colouring squares by counting
in **sixes**:

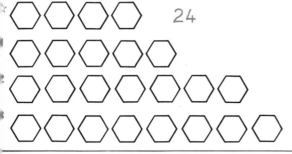

1	2	3	4	5	6	7	8	9	10
11	12	13	14	15	16	17	18	19	20
21	22	23	24	25	26	27	28	29	30
31	32	33	34	35	36	37	38	39	40
41	42	43	44	45	46	47	48	49	50
51	52	53	54	55	56	57	58	59	60
61	62	63	64	65	66	67	68	69	70
71	72	73	74	75	76	77	78	79	80
81	82	83	84	85	86	87	88	89	90
91	92	93	94	95	96	97	98	99	100

Count in **sixes**. Work out how many
corners on these hexagons:

☆ 24

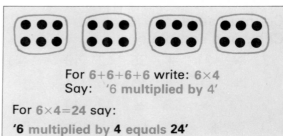

For **6+6+6+6** write: **6×4**
Say: '**6 multiplied by 4**'

For **6×4=24** say:
'**6 multiplied by 4 equals 24**'

D Multiply to find how many sides
altogether on these hexagons:

☆ 6×3=18
1
2
3
4
5

E Multiply to find how many faces
altogether on these cubes:

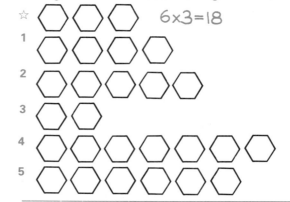

☆ 4×6=24
1
2
3

F Write numbers for ✳'s:

☆ 6×2=✳   12
1 6×3=✳   6 6×10=✳
2 6×5=✳   7 6×6=✳
3 6×4=✳   8 6×9=✳
4 6×7=✳   9 6×1=✳
5 6×8=✳   10 6×11=✳

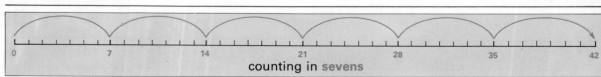

counting in **sevens**

A Count in **sevens**.
Copy and complete:

☆ 7 ✱ 21 ✱ 35 42 49
   7 14 21 28 35 42 49
1 7 14 ✱ 28 ✱ 42 49
2 0 7 ✱ 21 ✱ 35 42
3 0 ✱ 14 21 ✱ ✱ 42
4 7 14 ✱ ✱ 35 ✱ 49
5 0 ✱ ✱ 21 ✱ 35 ✱

B You need a hundred square.
Finish colouring squares by counting
in **sevens**:

1	2	3	4	5	6	7	8	9	10
11	12	13	14	15	16	17	18	19	20
21	22	23	24	25	26	27	28	29	30
31	32	33	34	35	36	37	38	39	40
41	42	43	44	45	46	47	48	49	50
51	52	53	54	55	56	57	58	59	60
61	62	63	64	65	66	67	68	69	70
71	72	73	74	75	76	77	78	79	80
81	82	83	84	85	86	87	88	89	90
91	92	93	94	95	96	97	98	99	100

C Count in **sevens**. Work out how many
sides altogether on these 50p coins:

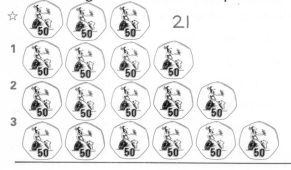

☆ 21

1

2

3

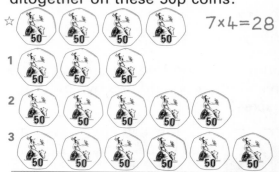

$7+7+7=21$
$7×3=21$
Say: '**7 multiplied by 3=21**'

D Multiply to find how many sides
altogether on these 50p coins:

☆ $7×4=28$

1

2

3

E Multiply to find how many petals
altogether on these flowers:

☆ $7×3=21$

1

2

3

F Write numbers for ✱'s:

☆ $7×4=$ ✱   28
1 $7×3=$ ✱   6 $7×10=$ ✱
2 $7×2=$ ✱   7 $7×6=$ ✱
3 $7×5=$ ✱   8 $7×9=$ ✱
4 $7×7=$ ✱   9 $7×8=$ ✱
5 $7×1=$ ✱   10 $7×11=$ ✱

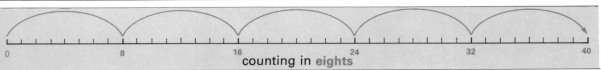

counting in **eights**

Count in **eights**.
Copy and complete:

☆ 8   *   24   *   40   *   56
8   16   24   32   40   48   56

1   8   16   *   32   *   48   56
2   0   *   16   *   *   40   *
3   16   *   32   *   48   *   64
4   8   *   *   32   *   48   *
5   0   8   *   *   32   *   *

You need a hundred square. Finish
colouring squares by counting in
eights:

1	2	3	4	5	6	7	8	9	10
11	12	13	14	15	16	17	18	19	20
21	22	23	24	25	26	27	28	29	30
31	32	33	34	35	36	37	38	39	40
41	42	43	44	45	46	47	48	49	50
51	52	53	54	55	56	57	58	59	60
61	62	63	64	65	66	67	68	69	70
71	72	73	74	75	76	77	78	79	80
81	82	83	84	85	86	87	88	89	90
91	92	93	94	95	96	97	98	99	100

Count in **eights**. How many legs
altogether on these spiders?

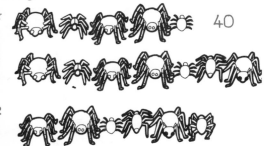

40

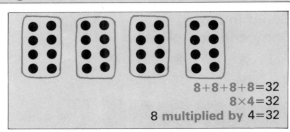

$8+8+8+8=32$
$8×4=32$
8 multiplied by $4=32$

D Multiply to find how many legs
altogether:

☆ $8×4=32$

1

2

E Multiply to find how many corners
altogether on these cubes:

☆ $8×3=24$

1

2

3

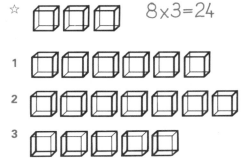

F Write numbers for *****'s:

☆ $8×5=$ *****   40

1 $8×3=$ *****   6 $8×7=$ *****
2 $8×6=$ *****   7 $8×8=$ *****
3 $8×2=$ *****   8 $8×1=$ *****
4 $8×4=$ *****   9 $8×9=$ *****
5 $8×10=$ *****   10 $8×11=$ *****

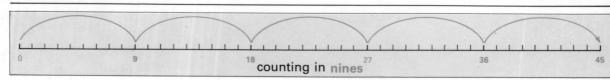

counting in **nines**

A Count in **nines**.
Copy and complete:

☆ 9   *   27   *   45   *   63
  9 18 27 36 45 54 63

1 9   18   *   36   *   54   63

2 0   *   18   *   36   45   *

3 18   27   *   *   54   *   72

4 0   9   *   27   *   *   54

5 9   *   *   36   *   *   63

B You need a hundred square.
Finish colouring squares by counting
in **nines**:

1	2	3	4	5	6	7	8	9	10
11	12	13	14	15	16	17	18	19	20
21	22	23	24	25	26	27	28	29	30
31	32	33	34	35	36	37	38	39	40
41	42	43	44	45	46	47	48	49	50
51	52	53	54	55	56	57	58	59	60
61	62	63	64	65	66	67	68	69	70
71	72	73	74	75	76	77	78	79	80
81	82	83	84	85	86	87	88	89	90
91	92	93	94	95	96	97	98	99	100

C Count in **nines**. How many studs
altogether on these boots?

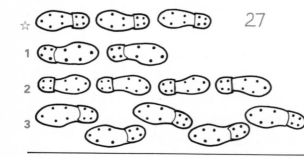

☆   27

1

2

3

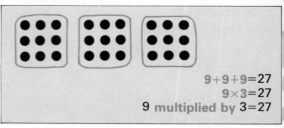

$9+9+9=27$
$9×3=27$
9 **multiplied by** 3=27

D Multiply to find how many people
altogether:

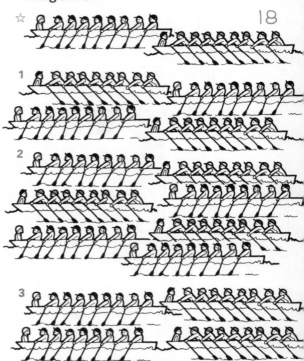

☆   18

1

2

3

E Write numbers for *'s:

☆ 9×4= *   36

1 9×6= *   6 9×10= *

2 9×2= *   7 9×8= *

3 9×5= *   8 9×9= *

4 9×3= *   9 9×1= *

5 9×7= *   10 9×11= *

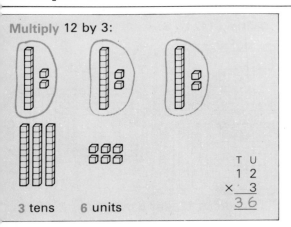

Multiply 12 by 3:

3 tens   6 units

```
T U
1 2
× 3
3 6
```

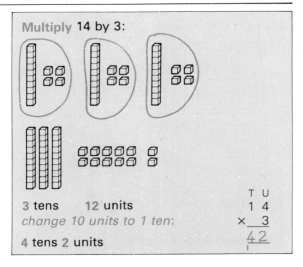

Multiply 14 by 3:

3 tens   12 units

change 10 units to 1 ten:

4 tens 2 units

```
T U
1 4
× 3
4 2
```

Use **multiplication** to find how many in each group:

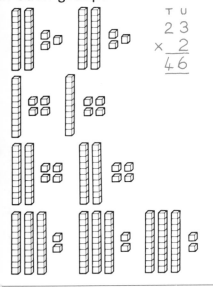

```
T U
2 3
× 2
4 6
```

C Use **multiplication** to find how many in each group:

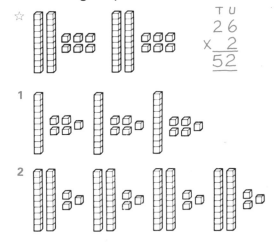

☆
```
T U
2 6
× 2
5 2
```

1

2

Copy and complete:

```
T U        T U
1 3        1 3
× 3        × 3
           3 9
```

```
T U      3  T U     5  T U
2 4         1 2        2 3
× 2         × 4        × 3
```

```
T U      4  T U     6  T U
3 3         2 2        1 3
× 3         × 4        × 2
```

D Use **multiplication** to answer these:

☆ Sweets are sold in bags of 16. How many sweets in 3 bags?
```
T U
1 6
× 3
4 8
```

1 Biscuits are sold in packets of 24. How many biscuits in 3 packets?

2 There are 24 bottles in a crate. How many bottles in 4 crates?

3 Crayons are packed in boxes of 14. How many crayons in 4 boxes?

4 There are 25 nails in each packet. How many nails in 3 packets?

Multiply 136 by 2:

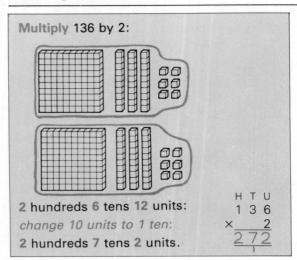

2 hundreds 6 tens 12 units:

change 10 units to 1 ten:

2 hundreds 7 tens 2 units.

```
  H T U
  1 3 6
×     2
  2 7 2
    ₁
```

Multiply 142 by 3:

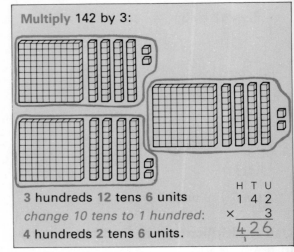

3 hundreds 12 tens 6 units

change 10 tens to 1 hundred:

4 hundreds 2 tens 6 units.

```
  H T U
  1 4 2
×     3
  4 2 6
    ₁
```

A Copy and complete:

☆
```
  H T U        H T U
  2 1 7        2 1 7
×     2      ×     2
            _____
              4 3 4
```

1
```
  H T U
  3 2 4
×     3
```

3
```
  H T U
  1 2 3
×     4
```

5
```
  H T U
  1 1 3
×     5
```

2
```
  H T U
  1 1 2
×     6
```

4
```
  H T U
  3 2 8
×     2
```

6
```
  H T U
  1 0 2
×     8
```

C Copy and complete:

☆
```
  H T U        H T U
  2 6 1        2 6 1
×     3      ×     3
            _____
              7 8 3
```

1
```
  H T U
  2 4 2
×     4
```

3
```
  H T U
  3 8 4
×     2
```

5
```
  H T U
  1 3 2
×     4
```

2
```
  H T U
  1 3 1
×     5
```

4
```
  H T U
  1 6 3
×     3
```

6
```
  H T U
  1 2 1
×     8
```

B Answer these questions:

☆ A factory makes 123 buckets each day. How many buckets are made in 4 days?　　　492

1 A machine washes 225 bottles each hour. How many bottles will it wash in 3 hours?

2 Four men are each paid £213 for a week's work. How much money is needed to pay all the men?

3 A lorry can carry 126 concrete blocks. How many blocks can the lorry deliver in three trips?

D Answer these questions:

☆ There are 164 flowers in each bed. How many flowers altogether in 3 beds?　　　492

1 There are 347 pages in each book. How many pages altogether in 2 books?

2 There are 152 seeds in each packet. How many seeds altogether in 3 packets?

3 There are 231 pins in a packet. How many pins altogether in 4 packets?

Multiplication

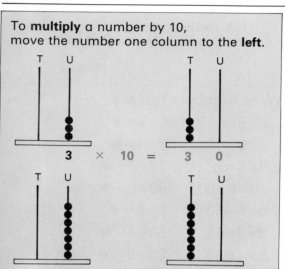

To **multiply** a number by 10, move the number one column to the **left**.

3 × 10 = 3 0

7 × 10 = 7 0

To divide a number by 10, move the number one column to the right.

4 0 ÷ 10 = 4

6 0 ÷ 10 = 6

Multiply by **10** the number shown on each abacus. Draw an abacus to show each answer:

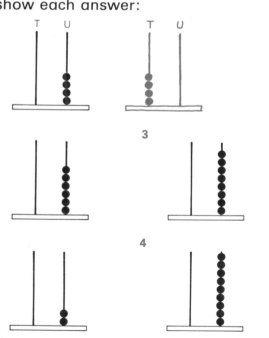

3

4

C **Divide** by **10** the number shown on each abacus. Draw an abacus to show each answer:

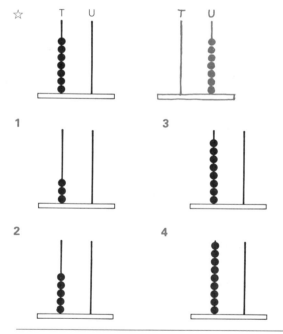

☆

1

2

3

4

Write numbers for **'s:

6×10= *   60

2×10= *   4 7×10= *

5×10= *   5 4×10= *

9×10= *   6 10×10= *

D Write numbers for **'s:

☆ 80÷10= *   8

1 40÷10= *   4 60÷10= *

2 20÷10= *   5 90÷10= *

3 70÷10= *   6 100÷10= *

This pattern of counters shows that:

$6×5=30$ $30÷6=5$
$5×6=30$ $30÷5=6$

A Write numbers for ✳'s:

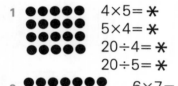

☆ $7×4=$ ✳   28
$4×7=$ ✳   28
$28÷$ ✳ $=7$ 4
$28÷7=$ ✳   4

1 $4×5=$ ✳
$5×4=$ ✳
$20÷4=$ ✳
$20÷5=$ ✳

2 $6×7=$ ✳
$7×6=$ ✳
$42÷6=$ ✳
$42÷$ ✳ $=6$

3 $8×4=$ ✳
$4×8=$ ✳
✳ $÷8=4$
$32÷4=$ ✳

4 $3×7=$ ✳
$7×3=$ ✳
$21÷7=$ ✳
$21÷$ ✳ $=7$

B Use counters if you need to.
Write numbers for ✳'s:

☆ $8×3=$ ✳   24
$3×8=$ ✳   24
$24÷8=$ ✳   3
$24÷$ ✳ $=8$ 3

1 $7×5=$ ✳
$5×7=$ ✳
$35÷5=$ ✳
$35÷7=$ ✳

2 $8×6=$ ✳
$6×8=$ ✳
$48÷8=$ ✳
$48÷6=$ ✳

3 $10×5=$ ✳
$5×10=$ ✳
$50÷10=$ ✳
$50÷$ ✳ $=10$

4 $10×9=$ ✳
✳ $×10=90$
$90÷$ ✳ $=9$
✳ $÷9=10$

If you know that $7×6=42$
you also know that $6×7=42$
$42÷7=6$
$42÷6=7$

C Write numbers for ✳'s:

☆ $7×8=56$ $56÷7=$ ✳   8
1 $9×5=45$ $5×9=$ ✳
2 $9×8=72$ $72÷9=$ ✳
3 $10×6=60$ $60÷6=$ ✳
4 $5×8=40$ $8×5=$ ✳
5 $6×9=54$ $54÷6=$ ✳
6 $9×7=63$ $63÷9=$ ✳

D Use **division** to answer these
questions:

☆ Mr Brown has 32 flowers. He divided
them into 4 equal bunches.
How many flowers
in each bunch? $32÷4=8$

1 A piece of string is 18 metres long. It
is cut into 3 equal pieces. How long
is each piece?

2 Five men share £40. Each man is
given an equal amount. How much
does each man receive?

3 In seven netball teams there are 49
girls. How many girls in each team?

4 Books are bundled in tens. How
many bundles will be made with 80
books?

5 Teddy bears cost £4 each. How many
teddy bears can you buy for £36?

6 Sausages are packed in eights. How
many packs can be made with 56
sausages?

Taxi!

When the taxi reaches a green box it follows the
road with the correct answer. Where is the taxi going?

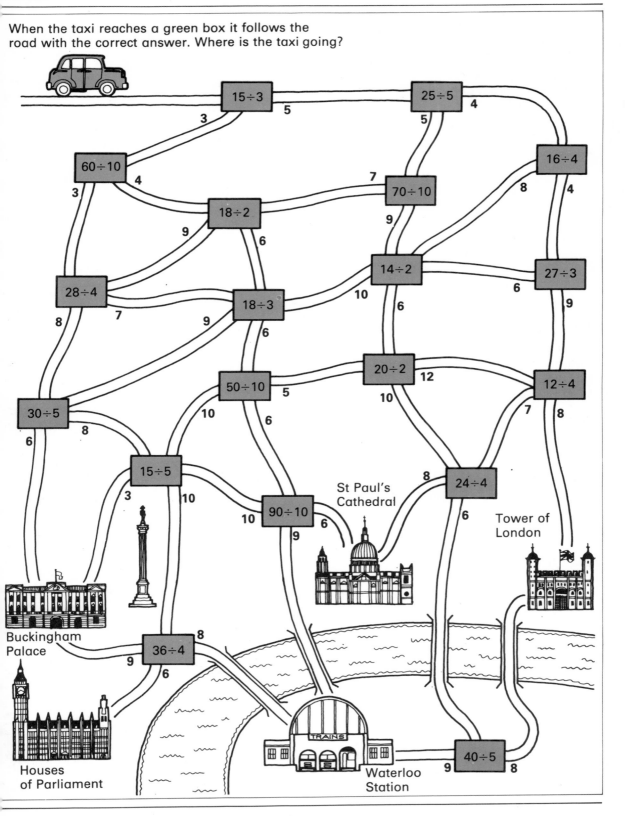

Divide **46** by 2:

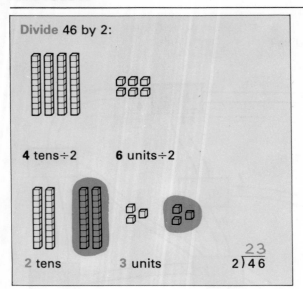

4 tens÷2   **6** units÷2

2 tens   **3** units $2\overline{)46}$ = 23

Divide 26 sweets equally between 2 children.
How many sweets each?

26 sweets $\overline{)26}$

2 children $2\overline{)26}$

13 sweets each. $2\overline{)26}$ = 13

How many bunches of 5 flowers can be made with 55 flowers?

55 flowers $\overline{)55}$

5 in each bunch $5\overline{)55}$

11 bunches can be made. $5\overline{)55}$ = 11

A How many in each group if you divide these tens and units into:

☆ 3 equal groups?

 $3\overline{)39}$ = 13

1 2 equal groups?   3 3 equal groups?

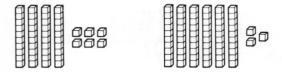

2 4 equal groups?   4 5 equal groups?

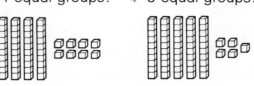

B Copy and complete:

☆ $4\overline{)48}$ $4\overline{)48}$ = 12

1 $3\overline{)36}$ 4 $4\overline{)84}$ 7 $5\overline{)50}$

2 $5\overline{)55}$ 5 $3\overline{)96}$ 8 $4\overline{)44}$

3 $2\overline{)68}$ 6 $2\overline{)82}$ 9 $6\overline{)60}$

C Answer these questions by **dividing**:

☆ Share 36 chips equally among 3 children.
How many chips each? $3\overline{)36}$ = 12

1 Divide 50 bananas equally among 5 monkeys. How many bananas each?

2 Divide 66p equally among 3 people. How much each?

3 Share 28 balloons equally between 2 children. How many balloons each?

4 Divide 84p equally among 4 people. How much each?

5 Ice creams are packed in fives. How many packs can be made with 55 ice creams?

CRICKET SET

6 Cricket sets have 2 bats. How many sets are made when 68 bats are used?

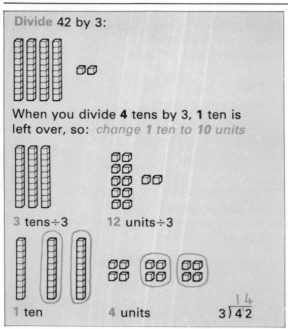

Divide 42 by 3:

When you divide **4** tens by 3, **1** ten is left over, so: *change 1 ten to 10 units*

3 tens÷3   12 units÷3

1 ten   4 units $3\overline{)4\,2}$ = 14

Divide 65 flowers equally among 5 flower beds. How many flowers in each bed?

65 flowers $\overline{)6\,5}$

5 beds $5\overline{)6\,5}$

13 flowers in each bed. $5\overline{)6\,5}$ = 13

Dice are packed in fours. How many packs can be made with 96 dice?

96 dice $\overline{)9\,6}$

4 in each pack $4\overline{)9\,6}$

24 packs can be made. $4\overline{)9\,6}$ = 24

A How many in each group if you divide these tens and units into:

☆ 2 equal groups?

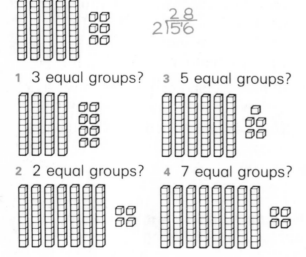

$2\overline{)5\,6}$ = 28

1 3 equal groups?   3 5 equal groups?

2 2 equal groups?   4 7 equal groups?

B Copy and complete:

☆ $3\overline{)7\,8}$ = 26

1 $3\overline{)4\,5}$ 4 $2\overline{)9\,6}$ 7 $2\overline{)7\,6}$

2 $4\overline{)5\,2}$ 5 $7\overline{)8\,4}$ 8 $3\overline{)7\,8}$

3 $5\overline{)6\,5}$ 6 $6\overline{)7\,8}$ 9 $4\overline{)9\,6}$

C Answer these questions:

☆ Divide 56 fish equally among 4 seals. How many fish each? $4\overline{)5\,6}$ = 14

1 Divide 45 sweets equally among 3 children. How many sweets each?

2 Share 60 felt pens equally among 5 children. How many pens each?

3 Sweets are packed in bags of 3. How many bags can be filled with 78 sweets?

4 Eggs are packed in sixes. How many packs can be made with 78 eggs?

5 There are 4 wheels on each car. How many cars are made when 92 wheels are used?

6 There are 5 crayons in each box. How many boxes can be filled with 60 crayons?

7 2 eyes are fitted to each doll. How many dolls are made when 94 eyes are fitted?

Write numbers for *'s:

6×3=*   7 6×*=30
7×4=*   8 7×*=35
8×6=*   9 9×*=81
10×7=*   10 8×*=56
5×8=*   11 4×*=36
9×6=*   12 9×*=72

Copy and complete:

```
    4 3        4      2 4     7     2 6 1
  ×   2             ×   4           ×     3

    2 6        5    1 3 2     8     1 3 1
  ×   2             ×   3           ×     6

    1 3        6    1 2 3     9     1 0 2
  ×   4             ×   4           ×     7
```

Answer these questions:

Packets contain 16 sausages. How many sausages in 3 packets?

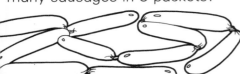

There are 14 screws in a pack. How many screws in 4 packs?

There are 124 nails in a box. How many nails in 3 boxes?

There are 39 flowers in a bunch. How many flowers in 2 bunches?

Spider aeroplanes carry 103 passengers. How many passengers can be carried on 6 of their planes?

D Write numbers for *'s:

1 24÷4=*   7 42÷7=*
2 27÷9=*   8 48÷6=*
3 36÷4=*   9 54÷9=*
4 60÷10=*   10 90÷10=*
5 30÷5=*   11 72÷9=*
6 24÷6=*   12 64÷8=*

E Copy and complete:

1 3)39   4 4)86   7 6)72

2 4)84   5 5)58   8 7)84

3 7)70   6 8)83   9 3)78

F Answer these questions:

1 In a football competition, there are 35 players in 7 teams. How many players in each team?

2

Share 48 chips equally among 4 children. How many chips each?

3 Divide 84p equally among 7 people. How much each?

4 49 worms are shared equally among 3 birds. How many worms does each bird get? How many are left over?

5 51 apples are packed in fours. How many packs are there? How many apples are left over?

6 Tins of beans are packed in boxes of eight. How many boxes can be filled with 94 tins? How many tins are left over?

Each of these cakes has been divided into **2** parts.

Only the middle one has been divided into 2 **halves**.

$\frac{1}{2}$ means **1** part of **2 equal parts**.

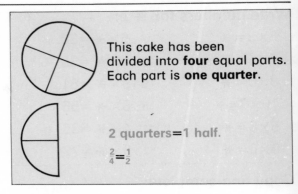

This cake has been divided into **four** equal parts. Each part is **one quarter**.

2 quarters=1 half.

$\frac{2}{4}=\frac{1}{2}$

A Have these cakes been divided into 2 **halves**? Write **yes** or **no**:

☆ yes

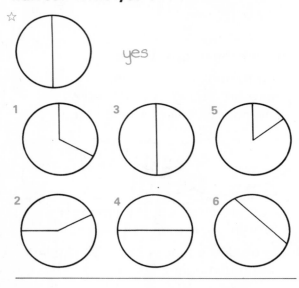

1   3   5

2   4   6

B Have these shapes been divided into **halves**? Write **yes** or **no**:

☆ yes

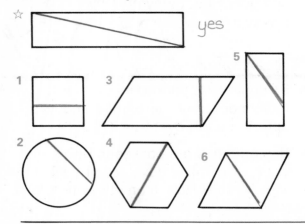

1   3   5

2   4   6

C Has one-half of each shape been shaded? Write **yes** or **no**:

☆ yes

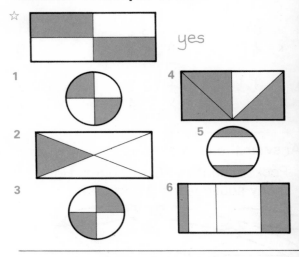

1   4

2   5

3   6

D What fraction of each shape has been shaded? Write $\frac{1}{4}$, $\frac{1}{2}$ or $\frac{3}{4}$:

☆ $\frac{3}{4}$

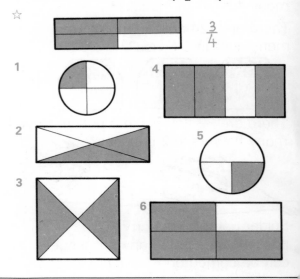

1   4

2   5

3   6

Fractions

shape	divided into	each part is called	write
○	2 equal parts	one **half**	$\frac{1}{2}$
○	3 equal parts	one **third**	$\frac{1}{3}$
○	4 equal parts	one **quarter**	$\frac{1}{4}$
○	5 equal parts	one **fifth**	$\frac{1}{5}$
○	6 equal parts	one **sixth**	$\frac{1}{6}$
○	8 equal parts	one **eighth**	$\frac{1}{8}$
○	10 equal parts	one **tenth**	$\frac{1}{10}$

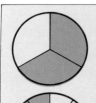

This shape is divided into **3 equal parts**.
2 parts are shaded.
$\frac{2}{3}$ of the shape is shaded.

This shape is divided into **10 equal parts**.
7 parts are shaded.
$\frac{7}{10}$ of the shape is shaded.

A Which of these shapes is divided into:

quarters?  b

thirds?

fifths?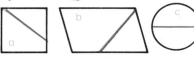

halves?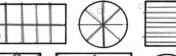

tenths?

eighths?

B What fraction of each shape is shaded?

☆ $\frac{5}{6}$

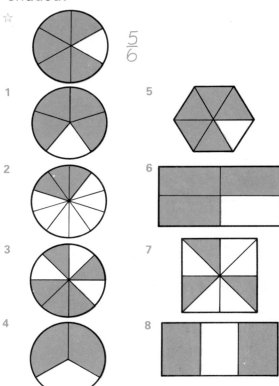

1

2

3

4

5

6

7

8

C Write in figures:

☆ three-tenths $\frac{3}{10}$

1 four-fifths
2 seven-tenths
3 five-eighths
4 two-thirds
5 three-quarters

6 nine-tenths
7 five-sixths
8 seven-eighths
9 three-fifths
10 three-eighths

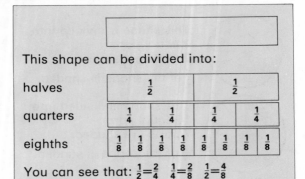

This shape can be divided into:

halves	$\frac{1}{2}$		$\frac{1}{2}$	
quarters	$\frac{1}{4}$	$\frac{1}{4}$	$\frac{1}{4}$	$\frac{1}{4}$
eighths	$\frac{1}{8}$ $\frac{1}{8}$	$\frac{1}{8}$ $\frac{1}{8}$	$\frac{1}{8}$ $\frac{1}{8}$	$\frac{1}{8}$ $\frac{1}{8}$

You can see that: $\frac{1}{2}=\frac{2}{4}$ $\frac{1}{4}=\frac{2}{8}$ $\frac{1}{2}=\frac{4}{8}$

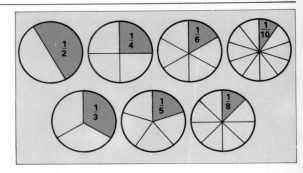

A

$\frac{1}{5}$	$\frac{1}{5}$	$\frac{1}{5}$	$\frac{1}{5}$	$\frac{1}{5}$

$\frac{1}{10}$	$\frac{1}{10}$	$\frac{1}{10}$	$\frac{1}{10}$	$\frac{1}{10}$	$\frac{1}{10}$	$\frac{1}{10}$	$\frac{1}{10}$	$\frac{1}{10}$	$\frac{1}{10}$

Copy and complete:

☆ $\frac{2}{5}=\frac{\ast}{10}$ $\frac{2}{5}=\frac{4}{10}$

1   $\frac{1}{5}=\frac{\ast}{10}$ 4 $\frac{2}{5}=\frac{\ast}{10}$

2   $\frac{6}{10}=\frac{\ast}{5}$ 5 $\frac{5}{5}=\frac{\ast}{10}$

3   $\frac{4}{5}=\frac{\ast}{10}$ 6 $\frac{8}{10}=\frac{\ast}{5}$

B

$\frac{1}{3}$	$\frac{1}{3}$	$\frac{1}{3}$

$\frac{1}{6}$	$\frac{1}{6}$	$\frac{1}{6}$	$\frac{1}{6}$	$\frac{1}{6}$	$\frac{1}{6}$

Copy and complete:

☆ $\frac{2}{3}=\frac{\ast}{6}$ $\frac{2}{3}=\frac{4}{6}$

1   $\frac{1}{3}=\frac{\ast}{6}$ 3 $\frac{4}{6}=\frac{\ast}{3}$

2   $\frac{3}{3}=\frac{\ast}{6}$ 4 $\frac{2}{3}=\frac{4}{\ast}$

C

$\frac{1}{2}$		$\frac{1}{2}$	

$\frac{1}{6}$	$\frac{1}{6}$	$\frac{1}{6}$	$\frac{1}{6}$	$\frac{1}{6}$	$\frac{1}{6}$

$\frac{1}{10}$	$\frac{1}{10}$	$\frac{1}{10}$	$\frac{1}{10}$	$\frac{1}{10}$	$\frac{1}{10}$	$\frac{1}{10}$	$\frac{1}{10}$	$\frac{1}{10}$	$\frac{1}{10}$

Copy and complete:

☆ $\frac{1}{2}=\frac{\ast}{6}$ $\frac{1}{2}=\frac{3}{6}$

1   $\frac{1}{2}=\frac{\ast}{10}$ 2 $\frac{3}{6}=\frac{\ast}{10}$ 3 $\frac{6}{6}=\frac{\ast}{10}$

D Write the sign < or > for ✶'s:

☆ $\frac{1}{5} \ast \frac{1}{10}$ >

1   $\frac{1}{3} \ast \frac{1}{6}$ 6 $\frac{2}{3} \ast \frac{2}{5}$

2   $\frac{1}{8} \ast \frac{1}{4}$ 7 $\frac{3}{6} \ast \frac{3}{10}$

3   $\frac{1}{2} \ast \frac{1}{5}$ 8 $\frac{5}{8} \ast \frac{1}{4}$

4   $\frac{1}{4} \ast \frac{1}{2}$ 9 $\frac{1}{3} \ast \frac{9}{10}$

5   $\frac{1}{10} \ast \frac{1}{5}$ 10 $\frac{1}{2} \ast \frac{3}{4}$

E Write numbers for ✶'s:

☆ 1 whole = ✶ quarters   4

1   1 whole = ✶ halves

2   1 whole = ✶ thirds

3   1 whole = ✶ fifths

4   1 whole = ✶ sixths

5   1 whole = ✶ eighths

6   1 whole = ✶ tenths

F What fraction of the cake have these children eaten?

	name	cake	fraction left	fraction eaten
☆	John	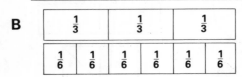	$\frac{4}{5}$	$\frac{1}{5}$
1	Alice		$\frac{2}{3}$	✶
2	Jim		$\frac{5}{8}$	✶
3	Mary		$\frac{3}{5}$	✶
4	Fred	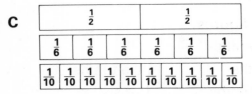	$\frac{1}{10}$	✶

Divide **67** by 2:

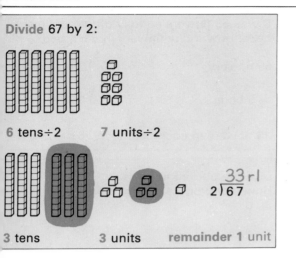

6 tens÷2   7 units÷2

$$\frac{33\,r1}{2\overline{)67}}$$

3 tens   3 units   remainder 1 unit

Divide into equal groups. How many in each group? How many left over?

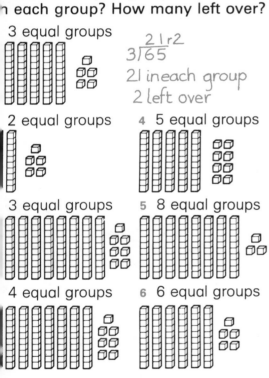

3 equal groups

$$\frac{2\,1\,r2}{3\overline{)65}}$$

21 in each group
2 left over

2 equal groups   4 5 equal groups

3 equal groups   5 8 equal groups

4 equal groups   6 6 equal groups

Copy and complete:

3)32 $$\frac{1\,0\,r2}{3\overline{)32}}$$

4)47   4 7)72   7 4)86

2)83   5 9)98   8 5)51

5)56   6 3)91   9 3)68

Share 25 buns equally between 2 elephants.
How many buns each?
How many buns left over?

25 buns   )25

2 elephants   2)25

12 buns each. 1 bun left $$\frac{12\,r1}{2\overline{)25}}$$
over.

Cakes are packed in fours.
How many packs can be made with
46 cakes?

How many cakes are left over?

46 cakes   )46

4 in each pack   4)46

11 packs. 2 cakes left $$\frac{11\,r2}{4\overline{)46}}$$
over.

**C How many each and how many left
over when:**

☆ 49 sheep are shared $$\frac{12\,r1}{4\overline{)49}}$$
equally among 4 farmers? 12 sheep each
                           1 left over

1 29 flies are shared equally between 2
spiders?

2 37 cakes are divided equally among 3
boys?

3 81 comics are shared equally among
4 girls?

**D How many packs and how many
apples left over when:**

☆ 37 apples are packed $$\frac{12\,r1}{3\overline{)37}}$$
in threes?   12 packs
                          1 left over

1 49 apples are packed in fours?

2 87 apples are packed in eights?

3 53 apples are packed in fives?

4 86 apples are packed in fours?

Fractions

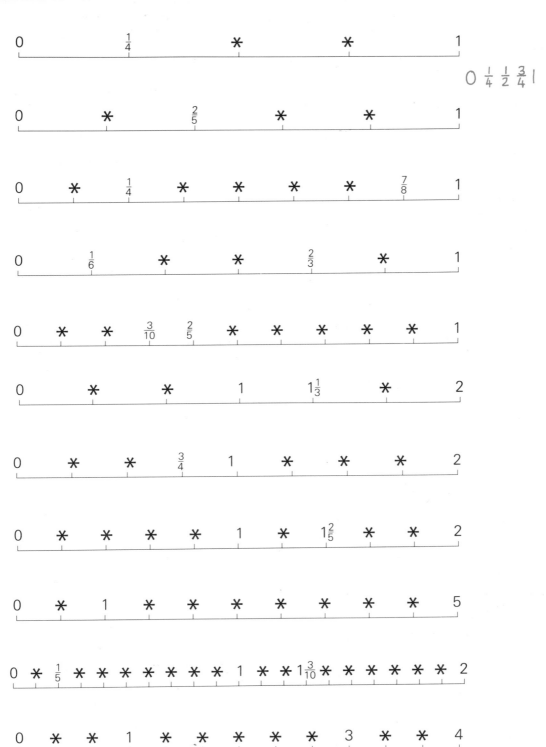

Copy the fractions on these number lines.
Write fractions for ✳'s:

0        $\frac{1}{4}$ ✳   ✳   1

$0 \;\; \frac{1}{4} \;\; \frac{1}{2} \;\; \frac{3}{4} \;\; 1$

0   ✳ $\frac{2}{5}$ ✳   ✳   1

0   ✳ $\frac{1}{4}$ ✳   ✳   ✳   ✳ $\frac{7}{8}$ 1

0        $\frac{1}{6}$ ✳   ✳ $\frac{2}{3}$ ✳   1

0   ✳   ✳ $\frac{3}{10}$ $\frac{2}{5}$ ✳   ✳   ✳   ✳   ✳   1

0   ✳   ✳   1 $1\frac{1}{3}$ ✳   2

0   ✳   ✳ $\frac{3}{4}$ 1   ✳   ✳   ✳   2

0   ✳   ✳   ✳   ✳   1   ✳ $1\frac{2}{5}$ ✳   ✳   2

0   ✳   1   ✳   ✳   ✳   ✳   ✳   ✳   ✳   5

0 ✳ $\frac{1}{5}$ ✳ ✳ ✳ ✳ ✳ ✳ 1 ✳ ✳ $1\frac{3}{10}$ ✳ ✳ ✳ ✳ ✳ 2

0   ✳   ✳   1   ✳   ✳   ✳   ✳   ✳   3   ✳   ✳   4

A There are **8** squares in this bar of chocolate.

How many squares in:

☆ $\frac{1}{2}$ a bar?   4

1 $\frac{1}{4}$ of a bar?   4 $\frac{3}{4}$ of a bar?

2 $\frac{1}{8}$ of a bar?   5 $\frac{5}{8}$ of a bar?

3 $\frac{3}{8}$ of a bar?   6 $\frac{7}{8}$ of a bar?

B There are **6** triangles in this hexagon.

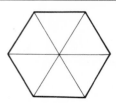

How many triangles make up:

☆ $\frac{1}{6}$ of the hexagon? |

1 $\frac{1}{3}$ of the hexagon?

2 $\frac{5}{6}$ of the hexagon?

3 $\frac{3}{6}$ of the hexagon?

4 $\frac{1}{2}$ of the hexagon?

5 $\frac{2}{3}$ of the hexagon?

6 $\frac{6}{6}$ of the hexagon?

C There are **10** sweets in a pack.

How many sweets in:

☆ $\frac{3}{10}$ of a pack?   3

1 $\frac{1}{10}$ of a pack?   5 $\frac{9}{10}$ of a pack?

2 $\frac{1}{5}$ of a pack?   6 $\frac{3}{5}$ of a pack?

3 $\frac{3}{10}$ of a pack?   7 $\frac{1}{2}$ of a pack?

4 $\frac{2}{5}$ of a pack?   8 $\frac{4}{5}$ of a pack?

There are **10** squares in this shape.
How many squares in half of the shape?

$\frac{1}{2}$ **of 10**$=5$

You can also find the answer by division:
10÷2=5

D How many squares in:

☆ $\frac{1}{4}$ of this shape?   2

1 $\frac{1}{8}$ of this shape?

2 $\frac{1}{5}$ of this shape?

3 $\frac{1}{3}$ of this shape?

4 $\frac{1}{10}$ of this shape?

5 $\frac{1}{2}$ of this shape?

6 $\frac{1}{6}$ of this shape?

E How long is:

☆ $\frac{1}{3}$ of this piece of string?

6 cm   2cm

1 $\frac{1}{4}$ of this piece of string?

8 cm

2 $\frac{1}{5}$ of this piece of string?

10 cm

3 $\frac{1}{10}$ of this piece of string?

10 cm

4 $\frac{1}{2}$ of this piece of string?

8 cm

Fractions

John eats half of these cakes:

How many cakes does he eat?

$6 \div 2 = 3$ $\frac{1}{2}$ of $6 = 3$

John eats **3** cakes.

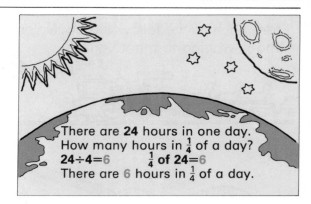

There are **24** hours in one day.
How many hours in $\frac{1}{4}$ of a day?
24÷4=6 $\frac{1}{4}$ **of 24=6**
There are **6** hours in $\frac{1}{4}$ of a day.

How many marbles in $\frac{1}{2}$ of each group?

☆    5

1

5

2

6

3

7

4

8

How many oranges is:

☆ $\frac{1}{3}$ of 12 oranges?   4

1 $\frac{1}{4}$ of 8 oranges?
2 $\frac{1}{5}$ of 15 oranges?
3 $\frac{1}{3}$ of 15 oranges?
4 $\frac{1}{6}$ of 18 oranges?
5 $\frac{1}{10}$ of 30 oranges?
6 $\frac{1}{8}$ of 16 oranges?
7 $\frac{1}{2}$ of 20 oranges?
8 $\frac{1}{10}$ of 100 oranges?
9 $\frac{1}{6}$ of 24 oranges?
10 $\frac{1}{5}$ of 30 oranges?
11 $\frac{1}{8}$ of 24 oranges?
12 $\frac{1}{3}$ of 24 oranges?

C Answer these questions:

☆ How many hours in $\frac{1}{3}$ of a day? $24 \div 3 = 8$

1 How many hours in $\frac{1}{2}$ a day?
2 How many hours in $\frac{1}{8}$ of a day?
3 How many hours in $\frac{1}{6}$ of a day?

D There are 30 days in September. Answer these questions:

☆ How many days in $\frac{1}{2}$ of September? $30 \div 2 = 15$

1 How many days in $\frac{1}{5}$ of September?
2 How many days in $\frac{1}{10}$ of September?
3 How many days in $\frac{1}{3}$ of September?
4 How many days in $\frac{1}{6}$ of September?

E    There are 60 minutes in 1 hour.

Answer these questions:

☆ How many minutes in $\frac{1}{2}$ an hour? $60 \div 2 = 30$

1 How many minutes in $\frac{1}{6}$ of an hour?
2 How many minutes in $\frac{1}{4}$ of an hour?
3 How many minutes in $\frac{1}{3}$ of an hour?
4 How many minutes in $\frac{1}{10}$ of an hour?
5 How many minutes in $\frac{1}{5}$ of an hour?

From each circle, follow the equivalent fraction.
Who is waiting to meet you?

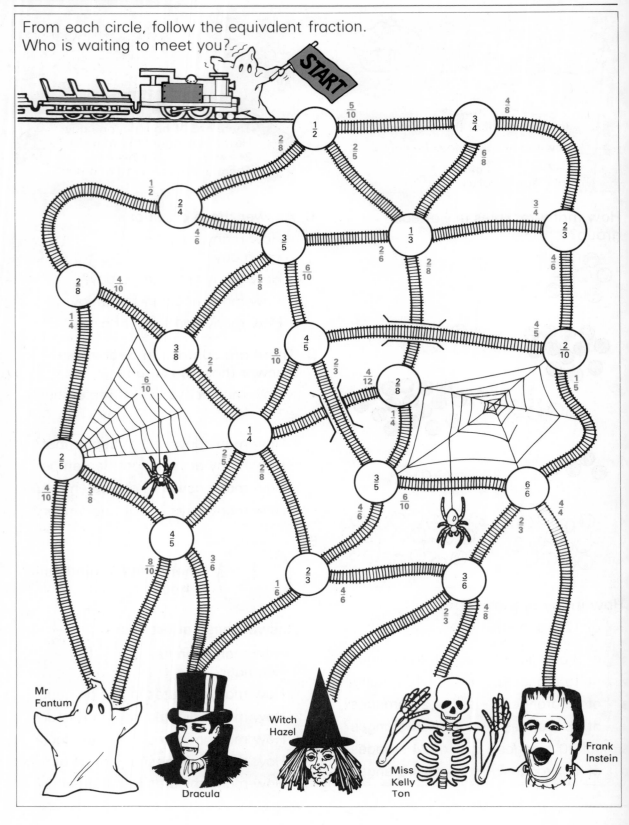

Mr Fantum

Dracula

Witch Hazel

Miss Kelly Ton

Frank Instein

What fraction of each shape has been coloured?

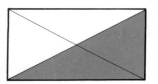

5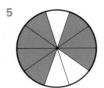

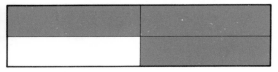

6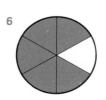

Write in figures:

one-sixth　　　　6 three-quarters

three-eighths　　7 five-eighths

seven-tenths　　 8 two-fifths

two-thirds　　　 9 five-sixths

four-fifths　　　10 three-tenths

Copy and complete:

$\frac{1}{3} = \frac{*}{6}$　　　　6 $\frac{2}{4} = \frac{1}{*}$

$\frac{1}{5} = \frac{*}{10}$　　　7 $\frac{1}{2} = \frac{4}{*}$

$\frac{8}{10} = \frac{*}{5}$　　　8 $\frac{2}{*} = \frac{4}{6}$

$\frac{5}{5} = \frac{*}{10}$　　　9 $\frac{6}{10} = \frac{3}{*}$

$\frac{3}{4} = \frac{*}{8}$　　　10 $\frac{4}{*} = \frac{8}{10}$

D How many beads in:

1 $\frac{1}{3}$ of this group?

2 $\frac{1}{4}$ of this group?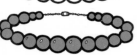

3 $\frac{1}{6}$ of this group?

4 $\frac{1}{10}$ of this group?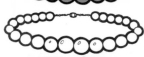

5 $\frac{1}{8}$ of this group?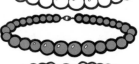

E Answer these questions:

1 Ben has 28 coins. Dan has $\frac{1}{4}$ as many. How many coins does Dan have?

2 David planted 56 tulip bulbs. $\frac{1}{8}$ of them did not grow. How many did not grow?

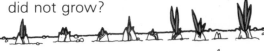

3 Jess had 60 sweets and ate $\frac{1}{10}$ of them. How many sweets did she eat?

4 $\frac{1}{6}$ of an archer's arrows missed the target. If 42 arrows were fired, how many missed the target?

5 24 cars were in a race. If $\frac{1}{4}$ of them did not finish the race, how many cars was this?

6 There are 45 tiles on the wall. If $\frac{1}{5}$ of them have a pattern, how many tiles were patterns?

A Which of these shapes covers more **surface**? Write **green** or **black**:

☆

green

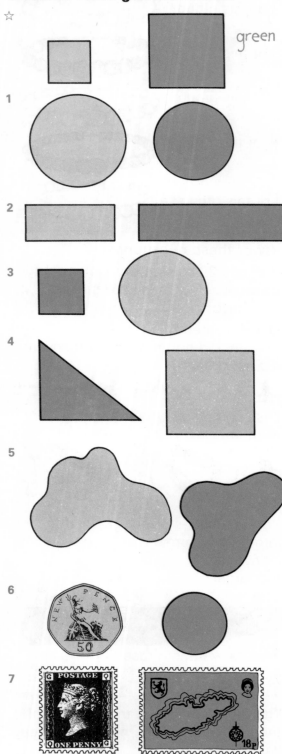

1

2

3

4

5

6

7

The **amount of surface** a shape covers is called its **area**.

B Which of these shapes has the smaller **area**? Write **green** or **black**:

☆

black

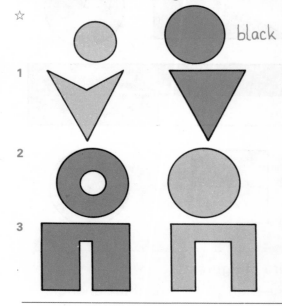

1

2

3

C Which of these shapes has the greater **area**? Write **green** or **black**:

☆

black

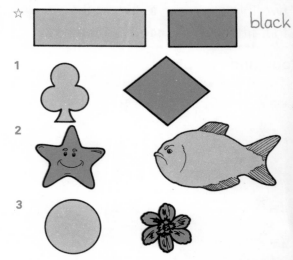

1

2

3

Area

Some shapes fit together leaving no **gaps**.

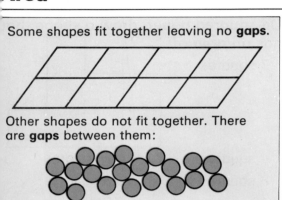

Other shapes do not fit together. There are **gaps** between them:

Use shapes if you need to.
Can you make a pattern
leaving no gaps using:

rectangles?

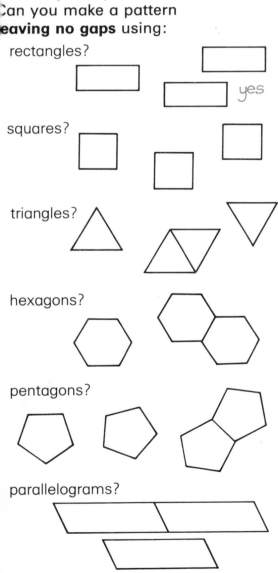

yes

squares?

triangles?

hexagons?

pentagons?

parallelograms?

B Which shape covers the larger **area**?
Write **green** or **black**:

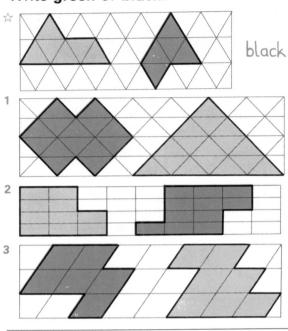

☆ black

1

2

3

C Which 2 shapes in each group have
the same **area**?

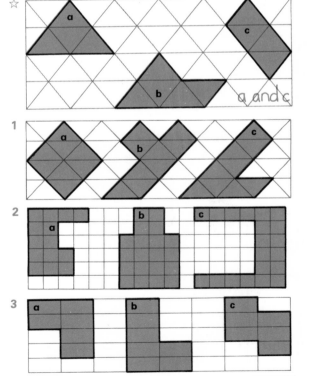

☆ a and c

1

2

3

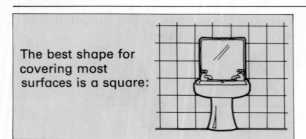

The best shape for covering most surfaces is a square:

A Write the area of these surfaces:

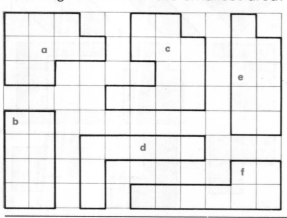

12 squares

B Which shape below has:

1 the largest area? **2** the smallest area?

C On squared paper, draw a shape that has an **area** of:

☆ 7 squares

1 4 squares	**6** 12 squares
2 8 squares	**7** 20 squares
3 10 squares	**8** 16 squares
4 1 square	**9** 11 squares
5 5 squares	**10** 25 squares

D On squared paper, draw 2 different shapes that both have an **area** of:

☆ 5 squares

1 3 squares	**6** 15 squares
2 7 squares	**7** 9 squares
3 10 squares	**8** 18 squares
4 6 squares	**9** 14 squares
5 11 squares	**10** 20 squares

E Which 3 shapes below have the same **area**?

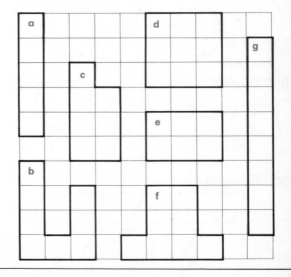

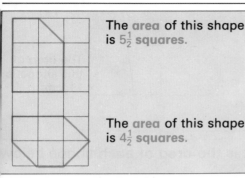

The **area** of this shape is $5\frac{1}{2}$ squares.

The **area** of this shape is $4\frac{1}{2}$ squares.

Write the **area** of these shapes:

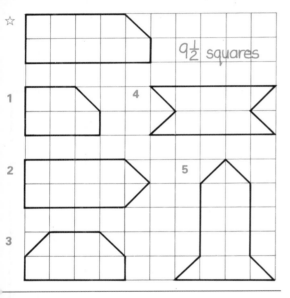

☆ $9\frac{1}{2}$ squares

1

4

2

5

3

Which shape has the larger **area**?

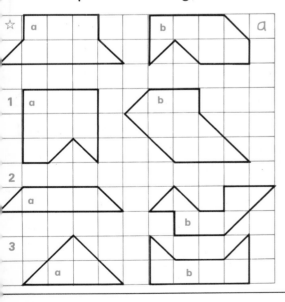

☆ a b

1 a b

2 a b

3 a b

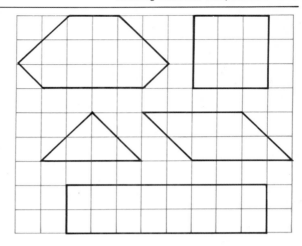

C What is the **area** of:

☆ the rectangle? 16 squares

1 the hexagon?   3 the square?

2 the parallelogram? 4 the triangle?

D On squared paper, draw a shape that has an **area** of:

☆ $9\frac{1}{2}$ squares

1 $5\frac{1}{2}$ squares   5 $10\frac{1}{2}$ squares

2 $2\frac{1}{2}$ squares   6 $16\frac{1}{2}$ squares

3 $7\frac{1}{2}$ squares   7 $12\frac{1}{2}$ squares

4 $3\frac{1}{2}$ squares   8 $20\frac{1}{2}$ squares

E Which 3 shapes below have the same **area**?

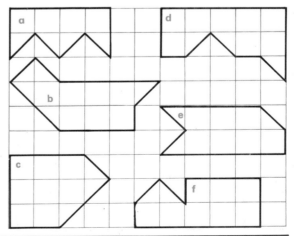

a   d

b   e

c   f

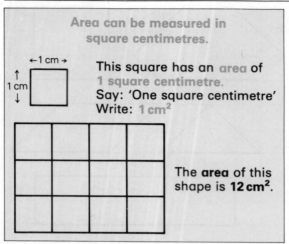

Area can be measured in square centimetres.

←1 cm→

This square has an area of 1 square centimetre.
Say: 'One square centimetre'
Write: 1 cm²

The area of this shape is **12 cm²**.

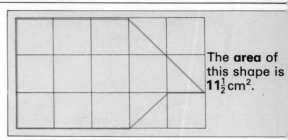

The **area** of this shape is **11½ cm²**.

A What is the **area** of each shape below?

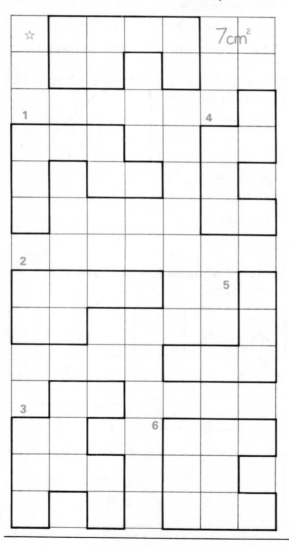

7cm²

B What is the **area** of each shape below

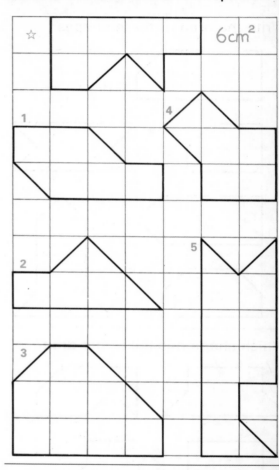

6cm²

C You need some centimetre squared paper.
Draw a shape that has an **area** of:

☆ 5½ cm²

1 8 cm²   3 10 cm²   5 3½ cm²
2 6 cm²   4 7 cm²   6 8½ cm²

Area

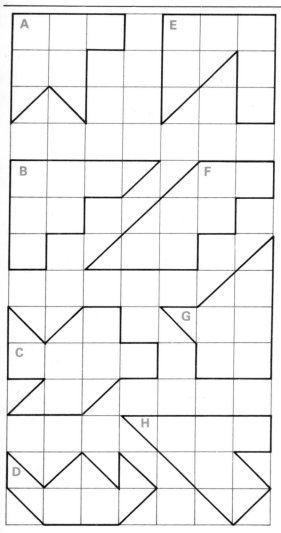

Write the **area** of each shape: A=6cm²

Which 3 shapes above have the same **area**?

You need some centimetre squared paper. Draw 2 different shapes that both have an **area** of:

4 cm²

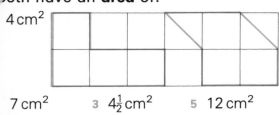

7 cm²   3 4½ cm²   5 12 cm²
10 cm²   4 8½ cm²   6 10½ cm²

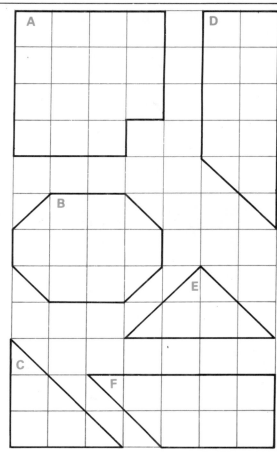

D Which shape above has:
☆ the largest area?   shape A
1 the smallest area?
2 the same area as shape B?
3 a greater area than shape D?
4 a smaller area than shape C?
5 an area of 4½ cm²?

E Use subtraction to find the difference in **area** between:
☆ shape A and shape F   7 cm²
1 shape A and shape B
2 shape B and shape F
3 shape E and shape B
4 shape F and shape E
5 shape E and shape A

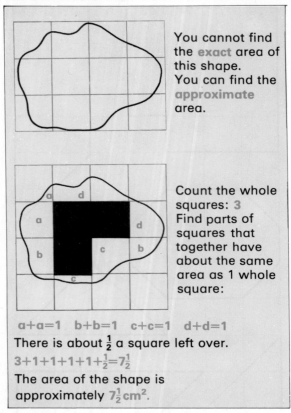

You cannot find the **exact** area of this shape.
You can find the **approximate** area.

Count the whole squares: **3**
Find parts of squares that together have about the same area as 1 whole square:

a+a=1   b+b=1   c+c=1   d+d=1

There is about $\frac{1}{2}$ a square left over.

$3+1+1+1+1+\frac{1}{2}=7\frac{1}{2}$

The area of the shape is approximately $7\frac{1}{2}\,cm^2$.

A Find the **approximate** area of these shapes:

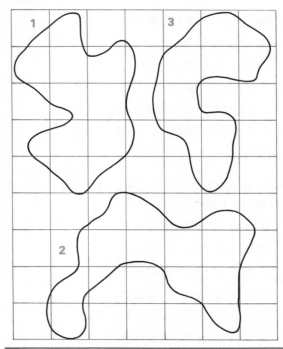

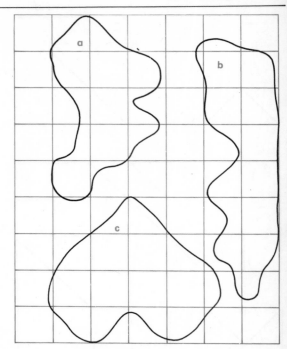

B 1 Which shape above do you think has the largest area?

2 Work out the area of each shape.

3 Did you choose the right shape in question 1?

C Work out the **approximate** area covered by this hand:

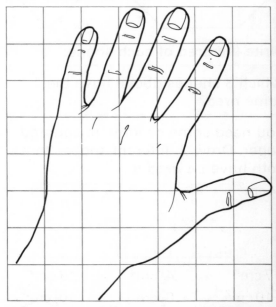

Area

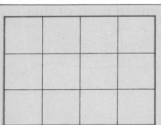

We can use multiplication to find how many squares in this rectangle. There are **4** squares in each row. There are **3** rows.

4×3=12

There are **12** squares altogether.
Each square has an area of **1 cm²**.
The **area** of the rectangle is **12 cm²**.

Use multiplication to find the areas of these rectangles:

$$5 \times 2 = 10$$
area 10 cm²

1

3

2

B Work out the area of each shape:

☆   14 cm²

1

2

3

A Write the area of each shape below:

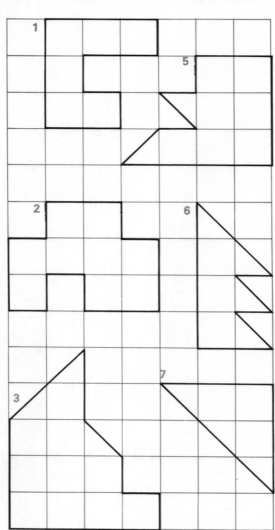

C Find the **approximate** area of this shape:

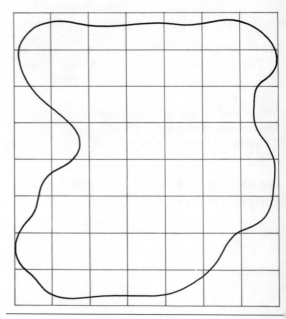

D Use multiplication to find the areas of these rectangles:

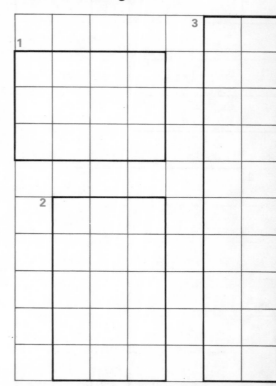

B You need some centimetre squared paper.
Draw a shape that has an area of:

1 6 cm²   3 5 cm²   5 9½ cm²

2 9 cm²   4 4½ cm²   6 11½ cm²

Counter attack!

1 You need 47 red counters and 29 green counters.
  (2 other colours will do.)
2 Work out the problem in each square.
3 Place red counters on squares with even number answers.
4 Place green counters on squares with odd number answers.

6×8	17+19	2⟌64		7×8	425 −143	10×10		8×4	910 + 62	54÷9
28 × 6	5×9	7×6		23+18	132 − 17	5⟌80		42÷6	5×5	4×9
314 −288	61 +58	12 × 8		3×7	5⟌55	28+16		443 −334	7⟌91	674 −138
57 +73	35−17	608 −196		47−8	5×7	9×6		9×9	18 +35	10×7
	10×5	9⟌90	24+38	56÷7		275 −197	63÷9	9×3	2⟌76	
	7×7	45÷5	265 −198	7×10		263 +175	46 +55	35÷7	7×4	
	23 +98	8×7	660 −192	6⟌96		8×8	8⟌80	5×4	426 +148	
	9⟌99	7×9	123 × 5	66+66		10×9	9×5	421 −100	8×9	
	9×8	4⟌96	72+58	42÷7		137 × 6	3⟌39	111 +112	75 × 4	

What do the counters say?

A How much money has:

☆ Sue? 89p

1 Bill?   3 Jim?

2 Helen?

B Name the person who has:

☆ less than 60 pence Jim

1 more than 95 pence

2 the most money

3 the least money

4 more money than Sue

5 less money than Bill

C Write the coins that could be used when:

☆ Jim spends 37p 20p 5p 5p 5p 2p

1 Sue spends 68p   5 Bill spends 25p

2 Helen spends 62p   6 Helen spends 72p

3 Bill spends 46p   7 Sue spends 74p

4 Jim spends 47p   8 Jim spends 17p

D Write the coins added to these amounts to make 50p:

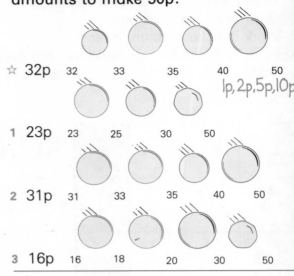

☆ 32p   32   33   35   40   50

1p, 2p, 5p, 10p

1 23p   23   25   30   50

2 31p   31   33   35   40   50

3 16p   16   18   20   30   50

E Write the coins added to these amounts to make £1:

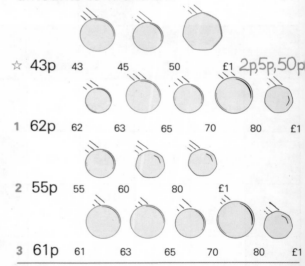

☆ 43p   43   45   50   £1   2p, 5p, 50p

1 62p   62   63   65   70   80   £1

2 55p   55   60   80   £1

3 61p   61   63   65   70   80   £1

F Copy and complete:

	cost	money given	change
☆	32p	50p	18p
1	29p	50p	
2	70p	£1	
3	16p	50p	
4	48p	£1	
5	32p	£1	

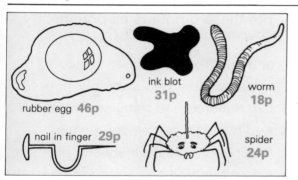

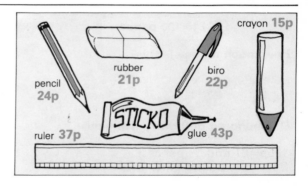

Find the cost in pence of:

☆ an ink blot and a worm   49p

1 a nail and a spider

2 an ink blot and a rubber egg

3 a rubber egg and a spider

4 a worm and a nail

5 a nail and an ink blot

6 an ink blot, a nail and a worm

7 a rubber egg, a spider and a worm

8 an ink blot, a nail and a spider

9 a nail, a worm and a spider

10 a rubber egg, a nail and a spider

Find how much you can save in the sale on:

☆ a mouse   ~~56p~~ 55p   31p

1 a peg doll   ~~97p~~ 82p

2 a pen   ~~75p~~ 59p

3 a ball   ~~53p~~ 38p

4 a book   ~~85p~~ 60p

5 a candle   ~~73p~~ 56p

6 cotton   ~~53p~~ 37p

C Work out the cost in pence of:

☆ 3 rubbers

$$\begin{array}{r} 21p \\ \times\ 3 \\ \hline 63p \end{array}$$

1 2 pencils   6 3 biros

2 2 tubes of glue   7 3 pencils

3 2 rubbers   8 2 rulers

4 4 rubbers   9 4 biros

5 2 crayons   10 3 crayons

D Answer these questions:

☆ If 3 needles cost 42 pence, what is the cost of 1 needle?

$$\begin{array}{r} 14p \\ 3\overline{)42p} \end{array}$$

1 If 2 thimbles cost 94 pence, what is the cost of 1 thimble?

2 If 4 crayons cost 56 pence, what is the cost of 1 crayon?

3 If 3 cakes cost 72 pence, what is the cost of 1 cake?

4 If 5 nails cost 60 pence, what is the cost of 1 nail?

5 If 2 comics cost 98 pence, what is the cost of 1 comic?

6 If 8 ribbons cost 96 pence, what is the cost of 1 ribbon?

7 If 7 pencils cost 91 pence, what is the cost of 1 pencil?

8 If 10 screws cost 80 pence, what is the cost of 1 screw?

£1=100 pence.

How much money is this?

One hundred and thirty-five pence.

135p=£1 and 35 pence.
Say: 'one pound thirty-five'
Write: **£1·35**

A Write these amounts in words:

☆ £1·45   One pound fortyfive

1 £1·82   5 £4·23
2 £6·30   6 £3·86
3 £2·51   7 £1·33
4 £1·97   8 £5·49

B Write these amounts as pounds:

☆

       £1·22

1

2

3

4

5

6

C Write these amounts as pounds:

☆ 237p   *£2·37*

1 one hundred and fifteen pence
2 three hundred and sixty-four pence
3 five hundred and thirty-seven pence
4 two hundred and eleven pence
5 four hundred and ninety-one pence
6 seven hundred and nineteen pence
7 six hundred and eighty-one pence
8 nine hundred and thirty-three pence
9 eight hundred and sixty pence
10 five hundred and forty pence

D Write these amounts as pounds:

☆ 354p   *£3·54*

1 242p   8 400p
2 471p   9 510p
3 386p   10 600p
4 854p   11 730p
5 739p   12 450p
6 617p   13 700p
7 999p   14 632p

E Copy this table.
Show the coins to pay each amount:

		£1	50p	20p	10p	5p	2p	1p
☆	£3·17	3			l	l	l	
1	£2·16							
2	£1·48							
3	£1·63							
4	£2·49							
5	£4·65							
6	£3·79							
7	£4·87							
8	£5·58							
9	£8·83							
10	£9·29							

You can write amounts in pounds:

Money:	Write:
	£0·03
	£0·64
	£1·17
	£1·06

Write these amounts as pounds:

£0·62

Write these amounts as pounds:

42p   £0·42

1 109p   4 260p   7 307p
2 111p   5 49p   8 1p
3 203p   6 80p   9 9p

C How many pence have the same value as:

☆ £1·38?   138

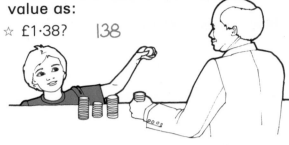

1 £2·32?   5 £1·49?   9 £0·09?
2 £1·65?   6 £0·08?   10 £1·10?
3 £2·80?   7 £0·76?   11 £1·90?
4 £3·07?   8 £0·90?   12 £0·19?

D How many 10p coins have the same value as:

☆ £0·50?   5

1 £0·30?   5 £2·00?   9 £2·40?
2 £0·40?   6 £3·00?   10 £3·10?
3 £0·90?   7 £1·20?   11 £4·50?
4 £1·00?   8 £1·60?   12 £5·80?

E Which is the larger amount of money?

☆ £1·37 or £1·73   £1·73

1 £1·65 or £1·56   7 £2·12 or £2·21
2 £2·11 or £1·89   8 £2·96 or £1·98
3 £2·64 or £4·26   9 £1·09 or £1·10
4 £1·01 or £0·99   10 £0·11 or £0·09
5 £0·86 or £1·05   11 £6·66 or £5·98
6 £1·01 or £1·10   12 £0·03 or £0·30

F Write these amounts as pounds:

☆ 600 pence   £6

1 400 pence   5 500 pence
2 200 pence   6 700 pence
3 300 pence   7 900 pence
4 100 pence   8 800 pence

58p+£1·23+£2·03

How much altogether?

Set out: £0·5 8
          £1·2 3
        +£2·0 3
Add: *£3·84*

You have: £2·64.
You spend: £1·35.
How much is left?

£2·6⁵4̇
−£1·3 5
£1·29

£1·29 is left

B How much is left when:

☆ you have £3·58 and
you buy a plate for £1·19?

£2·39

1 you have £4·28 and
you buy a book for £2·19?

2 you have £3·53 and
you buy a chess set for £2·37?

3 you have £5·82 and
you buy a pen for £1·79?

4 you have £6·55 and
you buy a bag for £3·38?

5 you have £4·40 and
you buy a torch for £2·15?

clown
94p

yo-yo
34p

plant
£1·64

doll
£2·02

vase
£1·35

tractor
£1·23

ball
£1·30

book
£1·18

C Copy and complete:

☆   £4·2 3
    −£1·0 7
    ————
            £3·16

1   £5·6 1   5   £7·6 1   9   £2·8 1
    −£3·2 7   −£1·5 8   −£0·3 6

2   £9·4 5   6   £3·9 1   10   £2·4 7
    −£1·2 8   −£1·0 2   −£1·6 5

3   £3·1 1   7   £4·4 4   11   £7·1 9
    −£1·0 7   −£1·1 9   −£3·6 6

4   £9·3 0   8   £6·5 0   12   £4·1 0
    −£2·6 2   −£0·2 8   −£2·5 2

**A How much do you spend when
you buy:**

☆ a clown, a ball and a yo-yo?

£0·94
£1·30
+ £0·34
————
£2·58

1 a ball and a plant?

2 a plant and a vase?

3 a tractor and a book?

4 a clown and a yo-yo?

5 a tractor, a doll and a ball?

6 a vase, a tractor and a doll?

7 a book, a tractor and a yo-yo?

8 a clown, a ball and a plant?

9 a doll, a plant and a book?

10 a vase, a book and a yo-yo?

11 a plant, a ball and a vase?

12 a clown, a tractor and a doll?

Write these amounts in words:

1 £1·46	6 £3·09
2 £1·98	7 £4·11
3 £2·60	8 £6·54
4 £3·20	9 £2·03
5 £4·88	10 £6·19

Write these amounts as pounds:

1

Write coins to pay these amounts:

1 £1·59	5 £3·06
2 £2·51	6 £1·99
3 £1·83	7 £0·83
4 £0·77	8 £2·64

The ornament shop

kingfisher £2·63

heron £4·24

crane £3·29

eagle £2·76

D 1 What is the total cost of a crane and a kingfisher?

2 What is the total cost of an eagle and a heron?

3 You have £4·37 and you buy a kingfisher. How much do you have left?

4 What is the difference in cost between a crane and a heron?

5 What is the total cost of a crane, an eagle and a kingfisher?

6 What is the total cost of 3 herons?

E Copy and complete:

1 £6·1 7 +£2·8 1		3 £4·2 5 +£2·6 8		5 £5·5 5 +£2·9 3	
2 £5·4 9 +£2·2 6		4 £9·5 1 +£0·3 9		6 £4·6 3 +£1·5 6	

F Copy and complete:

1 £3·6 9 −£1·3 7		3 £3·6 1 −£1·5 9		5 £4·7 1 −£2·8 0	
2 £4·8 3 −£2·3 4		4 £5·3 3 −£2·2 5		6 £6·3 7 −£5·9 2	

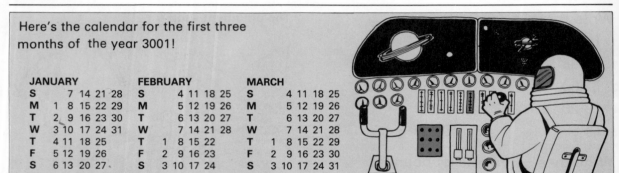

Here's the calendar for the first three months of the year 3001!

JANUARY						
S		7	14	21	28	
M	1	8	15	22	29	
T	2	9	16	23	30	
W	3	10	17	24	31	
T	4	11	18	25		
F	5	12	19	26		
S	6	13	20	27		

FEBRUARY					
S		4	11	18	25
M		5	12	19	26
T		6	13	20	27
W		7	14	21	28
T	1	8	15	22	
F	2	9	16	23	
S	3	10	17	24	

MARCH					
S		4	11	18	25
M		5	12	19	26
T		6	13	20	27
W		7	14	21	28
T	1	8	15	22	29
F	2	9	16	23	30
S	3	10	17	24	31

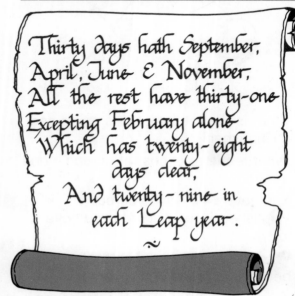

Thirty days hath September,
April, June & November,
All the rest have thirty-one
Excepting February alone
Which has twenty-eight
days clear,
And twenty-nine in
each Leap year.
~

A How many days in:

☆ a year?   365

1 September?   6 August?

2 June?   7 December?

3 January?   8 2 weeks?

4 July?   9 4 weeks?

5 March?   10 a leap year?

B Which month follows:

☆ March?   April

1 April?   6 August?

2 November?   7 January?

3 June?   8 September?

4 February?   9 May?

5 July?   10 December?

C What day of the year 3001 is:

☆ January 20th?   Saturday

1 February 20th?   5 March 11th?

2 March 15th?   6 March 6th?

3 January 3rd?   7 January 23rd?

4 February 28th?   8 February 18th?

D Which month of those shown has:

☆ 5 Wednesdays?   January

1 5 Tuesdays?

2 most Fridays?

3 Saturday on the 20th?

4 the last day on a Saturday?

5 the first day on a Monday?

E In the year 3001, what date is:

☆ the second Tuesday in March? 13th

1 the fourth Saturday in February?

2 the first Thursday in January?

3 the fourth Friday in March?

4 the third Sunday in February?

5 the second Wednesday in January?

F In the year 3001, what is the day:

☆ 5 days after 13th February? Sunday

1 3 days after 14th February?

2 7 days after 26th January?

3 2 days before 16th February?

4 8 days before 5th March?

Write these times:

quarter to 8

Draw clock faces to show these times:

¼ past 9

¼ to 3	4 ¼ past 2
half past 7	5 ¼ to 8
9 o'clock	6 half past 6

Write the time that is half an hour later than:

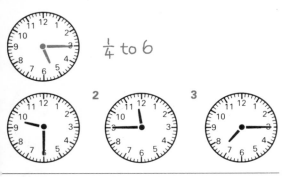

¼ to 6

Write the time that is ¼ of an hour earlier than:

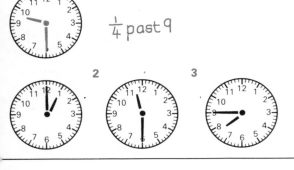

¼ past 9

What time is shown on this clock?

5 past
10 past
quarter past
20 past
25 past
half past

The **minute hand** is 20 minutes past the hour.
The **hour hand** is just past the 8.

The time on the clock is **20 minutes past 8.**
or **20 past 8.**

E Write these times:

5 past ten

F Draw clock faces to show these times:

☆ 10 past 6

1 20 past 4	4 5 minutes past 9
2 25 past 3	5 quarter past 10
3 10 past 11	6 20 minutes past 12

What time is shown on this clock?
The minute hand
is 20 minutes before the hour.
The hour hand is
nearly on the 4.

5 to
10 to
quarter to
20 to
25 to

The time on the clock is **20 minutes to 4**.
or **20 to 4**.

A Write these times:

☆

5 to 2

B Draw clock faces to show these times:
☆ 25 to 4

1 20 to 6   4 10 to 12
2 5 minutes to 3   5 25 to 9
3 quarter to 1   6 10 to 8

C Write these times:

☆

10 past 6

D What do you think you will be doing tomorrow morning, at these times?

☆

Write down the tim

sleeping

E What do you think you will be doing tomorrow afternoon at these times?

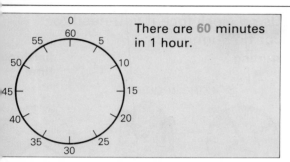

There are **60** minutes in 1 hour.

Count in **fives**.
Copy and complete:

0 5 * 15 * 25 *
0 5 10 15 20 25 30

0 * 10 * 20 25 *
15 * 25 * 35 * 45
20 * 30 35 * 45 *
30 * 40 * 50 55 *
25 * 35 * 45 50 *

How many minutes does it take for the **minute hand** to make:

$\frac{1}{2}$ turn?

30 minutes

1 full turn? 2 $\frac{1}{4}$ turn? 3 $\frac{3}{4}$ turn?

How long does it take for the **minute hand** to move from **a** to **b**?

15 minutes

  2   3

D Use a clock face if you need to.
For how long was:

starting time		finishing time

 ☆ John digging?

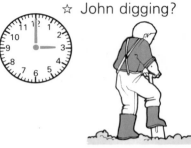 

I hour

1 Grandad sleeping?

2 the tortoise racing?

3 the rabbit burrowing?

4 the family eating?

5 the film showing?

A How long does it take for the **minute hand** to move from **A** to **B**?

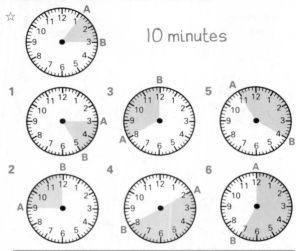

10 minutes

B Write the time that is **10 minutes later** than:

12 o'clock

C Write the time that is **20 minutes earlier** than:

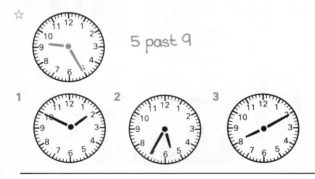

5 past 9

D Use a clock face if you need to.
For how long was:

| starting time | | finishing time |

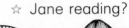

☆ Jane reading?

35 minutes

1 Bill driving?

2 Alec watching television?

3 the bat sleeping?

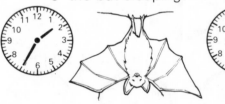

4 the bear's picnic?

5 the clown juggling?

How many days in:

April?   6 March?

July?   7 August?

May?   8 January?

June?   9 November?

October?   10 September?

JUNE						JULY					
S		6	13	20	27	S		4	11	18	25
M		7	14	21	28	M		5	12	19	26
T	1	8	15	22	29	T		6	13	20	27
W	2	9	16	23	30	W		7	14	21	28
T	3	10	17	24		T	1	8	15	22	29
F	4	11	18	25		F	2	9	16	23	30
S	5	12	19	26		S	3	10	17	24	31

What day is June 8th?

What day is July 16th?

What day is June 30th?

Which month has 5 Wednesdays?

Which month has the most
Saturdays?

Which month has its last day on a
Saturday?

What is the day five days after June
19th?

What is the day 6 days before July
15th?

What is the day 8 days after June
26th?

Write these times:

D Write the time that is:

1 $\frac{1}{4}$ of an hour
   earlier than

4 25 minutes later
   than

2 20 minutes later
   than

5 25 minutes
   earlier than

3 10 minutes
   earlier than

6 $\frac{1}{2}$ an hour later
   than

E For how long was:

starting   finishing
time   time

1 Sharon swimming?

2 Jo climbing?

3 Robin skating?

A Write how many altogether:

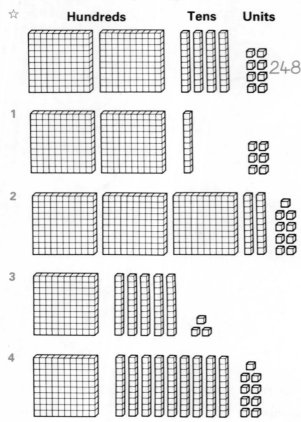

B Write in words:

☆ 345 three hundred and forty-five

1 327   5 260
2 185   6 402
3 436   7 109
4 190   8 601

C Write in figures:

☆ two hundred and fifty-three 253
1 four hundred and thirty-seven
2 nine hundred and eighty
3 six hundred and fourteen
4 five hundred and two
5 one hundred and eleven
6 nine hundred and nine

D Write the number shown on each abacus:

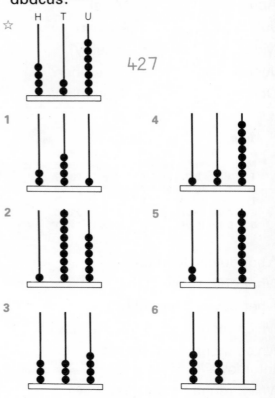

E How many packs of 10 sweets can be made from:

☆ 170 sweets? 17
1 140 sweets?   5 450 sweets?
2 260 sweets?   6 230 sweets?
3 110 sweets?   7 540 sweets?
4 300 sweets?   8 960 sweets?

F Arrange these numbers in order, **smallest first:**

☆ 327   183   496   692   175
   175   183   327   496   692
1 342   480   937   169   601
2 245   542   425   254   452
3 109   901   900   190   919
4 332   233   323   322   232
5 421   412   419   429   420

Place value

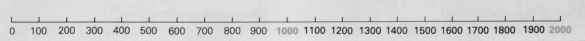

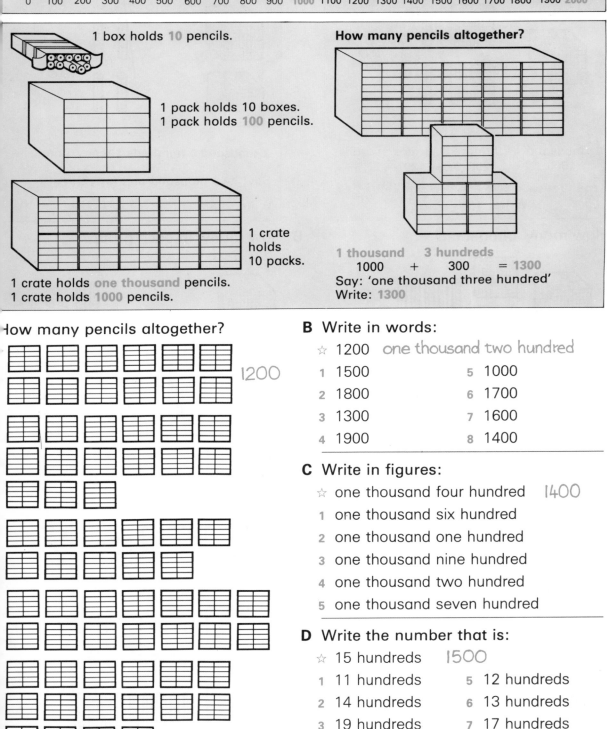

1 box holds **10** pencils.

1 pack holds 10 boxes.
1 pack holds **100** pencils.

1 crate
holds
10 packs.

1 crate holds **one thousand** pencils.
1 crate holds **1000** pencils.

How many pencils altogether?

1 thousand   3 hundreds
   1000   +   300   = **1300**
Say: 'one thousand three hundred'
Write: **1300**

How many pencils altogether?

1200

B Write in words:

☆ 1200 one thousand two hundred

1 1500   5 1000

2 1800   6 1700

3 1300   7 1600

4 1900   8 1400

C Write in figures:

☆ one thousand four hundred   1400

1 one thousand six hundred

2 one thousand one hundred

3 one thousand nine hundred

4 one thousand two hundred

5 one thousand seven hundred

D Write the number that is:

☆ 15 hundreds   1500

1 11 hundreds   5 12 hundreds

2 14 hundreds   6 13 hundreds

3 19 hundreds   7 17 hundreds

4 16 hundreds   8 10 hundreds

How many altogether?

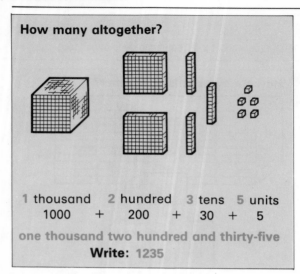

1 thousand   **2** hundred   **3** tens   **5** units
  1000   +   200   +   30   +   5

one thousand two hundred and thirty-five
Write: 1235

How many altogether?

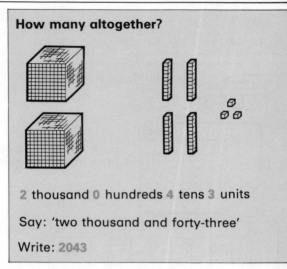

2 thousand **0** hundreds **4** tens **3** units

Say: 'two thousand and forty-three'

Write: **2043**

A How many altogether?

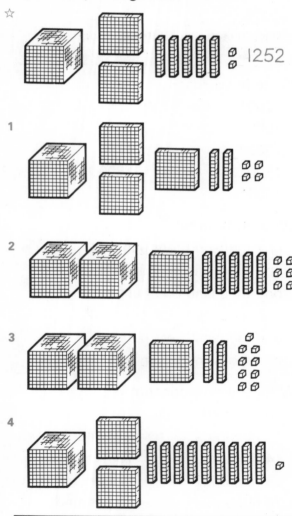

☆   1252

1

2

3

4

B How many in each group?

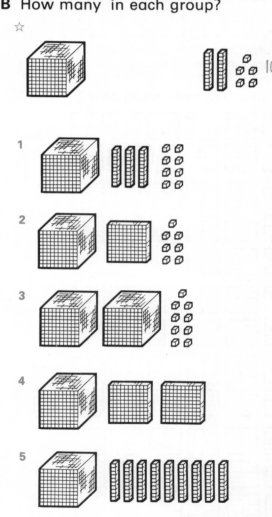

☆   1025

1

2

3

4

5

Place value

Write in figures:

☆ one thousand two hundred and four

1204

1 two thousand five hundred and fifty-one

2 one thousand two hundred and seven

3 one thousand six hundred and twenty

4 two thousand and forty-three

5 three thousand and ten

Write in words:

☆ 1210

one thousand two hundred and ten

1	2468	6	1506
2	1049	7	1052
3	2100	8	1930
4	3160	9	1424
5	4214	10	3001

Write these numbers in thousands, hundreds, tens and units:

☆ 1432

1 thousand 4 hundreds 3 tens 2 units

1	1579	6	2034
2	2645	7	4000
3	3109	8	2606
4	2640	9	3201
5	1091	10	4007

Write the number that is:

☆ 5 thousands 0 hundreds 1 ten 6 units

5016

1 1 thousand 7 hundreds 1 ten 4 units

2 2 thousands 9 hundreds 0 tens 2 units

3 4 thousands 0 hundreds 7 tens 0 units

4 2 thousands 2 hundreds 6 tens 1 unit

5 5 thousands 3 hundreds 0 tens 6 units

6 3 thousands 0 hundreds 5 tens 9 units

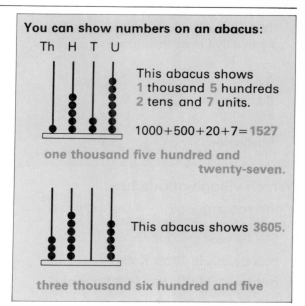

You can show numbers on an abacus:

Th H T U

This abacus shows
1 thousand 5 hundreds
2 tens and 7 units.

1000+500+20+7= 1527

one thousand five hundred and twenty-seven.

This abacus shows 3605.

three thousand six hundred and five

E Write the number shown on each abacus in 2 different ways:

☆

4218
four thousand two hundred and eighteen

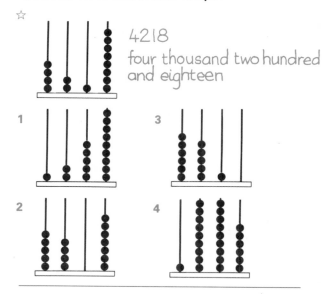

1

3

2

4

F Draw abacus pictures to show these numbers:

☆ 2437

1	1234	3	2463
2	1738	4	3806
		5	7650
		6	4021

The numbers in green show how many people live in each village.

village	population
Beer	1545
Bembridge	3281
Kegworth	2823
Kelso	5170
Rustington	8904

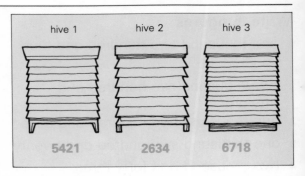

hive 1   hive 2   hive 3

5421   2634   6718

A Which village above has:

☆ the most people? Rustington

1 the fewest people?

2 more people than Kelso?

3 between 5000 and 6000 people?

4 more people than Kegworth but less than Kelso?

5 less than 2000 people?

B Work out the new population if:

☆ 8 people move in to Kelso   5178

1 10 people move in to Beer

2 7 people move in to Rustington

3 6 people leave Bembridge

4 7 people leave Kegworth

5 11 people move in to Kelso

C Arrange these mountains in order of height, **smallest first**:

mountain	height in metres
Kilamanjaro	5893
Ben Nevis	1344
Everest	8800
Mont Blanc	4813
Elbruz	5650
Cook	3766

D The **green** numbers show how many bees in each hive.
How many bees in the hive if:

☆ 20 bees join hive 1?   5441

1 10 bees join hive 3?

2 20 bees join hive 2?

3 40 bees join hive 3?

4 60 bees join hive 1?

5 100 bees join hive 3?

6 300 bees join hive 2?

7 500 bees join hive 1?

8 1000 bees join hive 3?

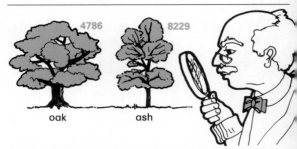

4786   8229

oak   ash

E The numbers in **green** show how many leaves there are on each tree.
How many leaves left on the tree if:

☆ 20 leaves fall from the oak tree? 4766

1 10 leaves fall from the ash tree?

2 70 leaves fall from the oak tree?

3 100 leaves fall from the ash tree?

4 400 leaves fall from the oak tree?

5 1000 leaves fall from the ash tree?

6 2000 leaves fall from the oak tree?

Write in words:

1 1400   6 1362
2 1900   7 1498
3 1600   8 3605
4 3100   9 2096
5 2500   10 4008

Write in figures:

1 one thousand eight hundred
2 four thousand two hundred
3 two thousand six hundred and fifty
4 nine thousand three hundred and eleven
5 seven thousand and seventy-seven
6 five thousand nine hundred and one
7 one thousand one hundred and one
8 nine thousand eight hundred and
   seventy-six

Write the number that is:

1 1 thousand 2 hundreds 5 tens and
   8 units
2 2 thousands 3 hundreds 6 tens and
   3 units
3 5 thousands 7 hundreds 5 tens and
   5 units
4 1 thousand 1 hundred 1 ten and 7 units
5 8 thousands 2 hundreds 0 tens 0 units
6 6 thousands 0 hundreds 2 tens 6 units
7 9 thousands 0 hundreds 6 tens 0 units
8 4 thousands 0 hundreds 0 tens 5 units

Write these numbers in thousands,
hundreds, tens and units:

1 1647   6 4706
2 2143   7 3201
3 6275   8 4017
4 1260   9 3028
5 2370   10 1007

E Write the number shown on each
abacus:

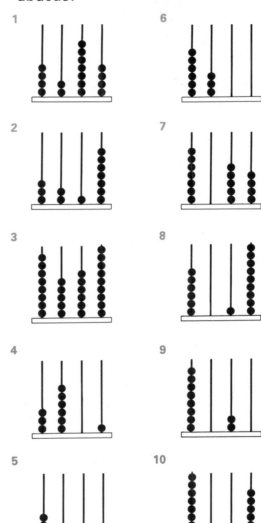

F Write these numbers in order,
smallest first:

1 6312   1796   4231   5760   9010
2 7436   8215   7869   8912   7777
3 3216   3719   3876   3914   3027
4 8195   8186   8126   8172   8107
5 4036   4010   4100   4063   4136
6 7676   6767   6777   7666   6776

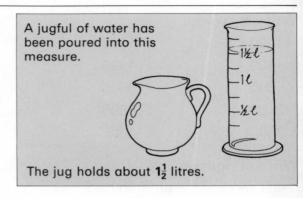

A jugful of water has been poured into this measure.

The jug holds about **1½ litres.**

A Which object above do you think would have a capacity of:

☆ 1 litre?   bottle

1 ½ litre?

2 15 litres?

3 30 litres?

4 600 litres?

mug holds ¼ litre

jug holds ½ litre

bottle holds 1 litre

vase holds more than 1 litre

tube holds more than ½ litre but less than 1 litre

B Answer these questions:

☆ How many mugfuls of water will fill the jug?   2

1 Which object has the greatest capacity?

2 Write the objects in order of capacity, smallest first.

3 Will water overflow when a tubeful of water is poured into the jug?

4 Will water overflow when a bottleful of water is poured into the vase?

5 How many mugfuls of water fill the bottle?

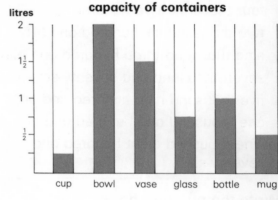

capacity of containers

litres

container

C Use the graph to answer these questions:

☆ Which container has the smallest capacity?   the cup

1 Which container has the greatest capacity?

2 Which containers have a capacity of more than $1\frac{1}{4}$ litres?

3 What is the difference in capacity between the bowl and the vase?

4 What is the total capacity of the mug and the vase?

5 If a mug of water is poured from the bottle, how much water is left in the bottle?

6 If a vase of water is taken from the bowl, how much water is left in the bowl?

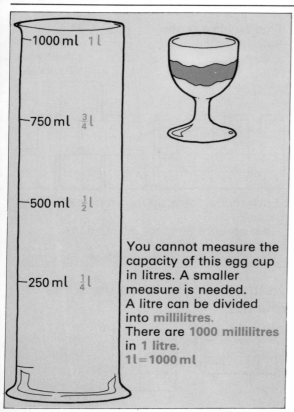

You cannot measure the capacity of this egg cup in litres. A smaller measure is needed.
A litre can be divided into millilitres.
There are 1000 millilitres in 1 litre.
1l = 1000 ml

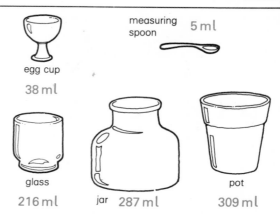

measuring spoon 5 ml

egg cup 38 ml

glass 216 ml

jar 287 ml

pot 309 ml

Write these capacities in millilitres:

☆ $\frac{1}{4}$l   250 ml

1 $\frac{1}{2}$l   4 5l

2 $\frac{3}{4}$l   5 1$\frac{1}{2}$l

3 2l   6 1$\frac{1}{4}$l

Write the sign < or > for *'s:

☆ 463 ml * $\frac{1}{2}$l   <

1 560 ml * $\frac{1}{2}$l   4 1326 ml * 1$\frac{1}{4}$l

2 965 ml * 1l   5 $\frac{3}{4}$l * 600 ml

3 200 ml * $\frac{1}{4}$l

Write these capacities in litres and millilitres:

☆ 2634 ml   2l 634 ml

1 1250 ml   4 5600 ml

2 1563 ml   5 4126 ml

3 2421 ml   6 1027 ml

D Work out the total capacity of:

☆ the jar and the glass   503 ml

1 the pot and the egg cup

2 the measuring spoon and the glass

3 the jar and the egg cup

4 the glass and the pot

5 the jar, the egg cup and the measuring spoon

6 the glass, the pot and the jar

E What is the difference in capacity between:

☆ the jar and the egg cup?   249 ml

1 the pot and the glass?

2 the egg cup and the measuring spoon?

3 the jar and the glass?

4 the jar and the pot?

5 the pot and the egg cup?

6 the glass and the egg cup?

F What would be the capacity of:

☆ 3 glasses?   648 ml

1 7 measuring spoons?

2 2 egg cups?

3 2 pots?

4 9 measuring spoons?

5 4 glasses?

6 3 pots?

John needs 20 cubes to build a block of flats.

Mary needs 15 cubes to build a factory.

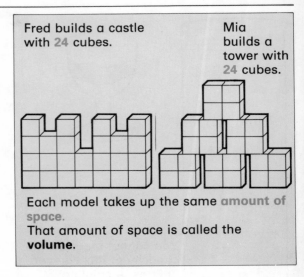

Fred builds a castle with **24** cubes.

Mia builds a tower with **24** cubes.

Each model takes up the same **amount of space**.
That amount of space is called the **volume**.

A Use cubes if you need to.
Work out how many cubes have been used to make each shape below:

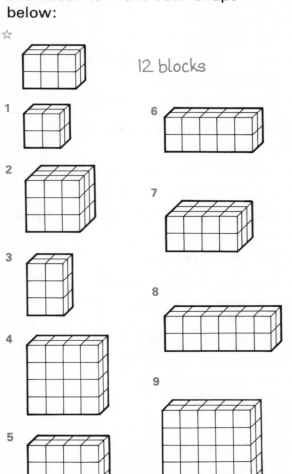

☆　　12 blocks

1

6

2

7

3

8

4

9

5

B Do these cuboids have the same **volume**?

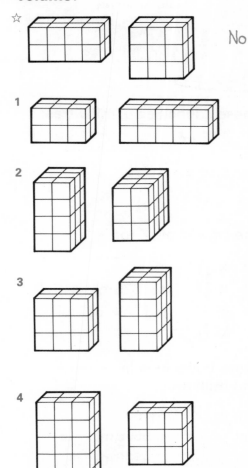

☆　　No

1

2

3

4

| 0 | 500 | 1000 | 1500 | 2000 | 2500 | 3000 | 3500 | 4000 | 4500 | 5000 | 5500 | 6000 | 6500 | 7000 |

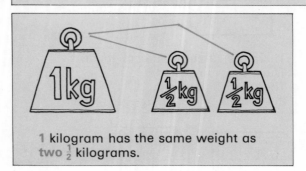

1 kilogram has the same weight as **two** $\frac{1}{2}$ **kilograms**.

You cannot measure the weight of this tennis ball in kilograms. A smaller measure is needed.

1000 grams have the same weight as **1 kilogram**.

$$1000\,g = 1\,kg \qquad 500\,g = \tfrac{1}{2}\,kg$$

A Write the weight of each object below:

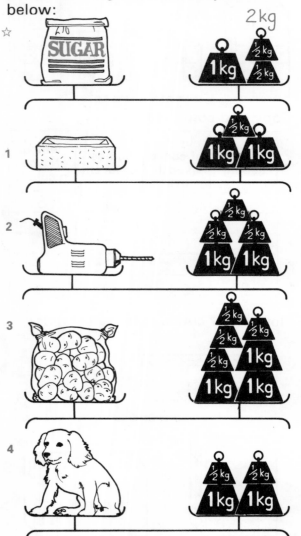

☆ 2kg

1

2

3

4

B Write the weights of these objects in grams:

☆ 1500g

1½ kg

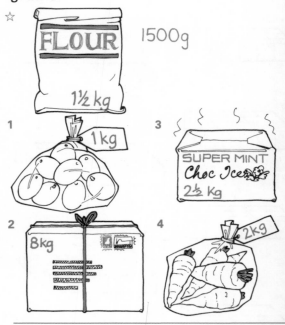

1

2   8kg

3   SUPER MINT Choc Ice 2½ kg

4   2kg

C Write these weights in order, **smallest first**:

☆ 2 kg 2500 g 1½ kg 3 kg
    1½kg 2 kg 2500g 3kg

1 1500 g 1 kg ½ kg 2000 g

2 2½ kg 3500 g 3 kg 1500 g

3 500 g 1½ kg 1000 g 2 kg

4 6000 g 7 kg 6½ kg 5500 g

5 5 kg 6500 g 5½ kg 6000 g

Weight

Use weights and scales if you need to. How many:

500 g weights balance 1 kg?　　2

100 g weights balance 1 kg?

100 g weights balance 500 g?

500 g weights balance 2 kg?

500 g weights balance 5 kg?

100 g weights balance $1\frac{1}{2}$ kg?

100 g weights balance 2 kg?

Write the total weight of each group in grams:

 800g

C Write weights that will balance each object:

☆ DOGO MUNCHY 1200g　　1kg 100g 100g

1 700 g

2 1300 g

3 900 g

4 1600 g

5 1800 g

6 1700 g

Harry Hamster 390 g

Gerry Gerbil 175 g

Gilbert Guinea Pig $\frac{1}{2}$ kg

Ricky Rabbit 1 kg

D Answer these questions:

☆ Which pet is lightest?　Gerry Gerbil

1 Which pet is heaviest?

2 Which pets weigh more than 450 g?

3 Write the pets in order of weight, lightest first.

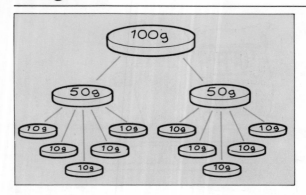

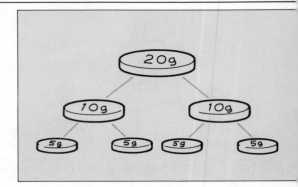

A Use weights and scales if you need to. How many:

☆ 50 g weights balance 1 kg?   20

1 50 g weights balance $\frac{1}{2}$ kg?

2 10 g weights balance 50 g?

3 10 g weights balance 100 g?

4 50 g weights balance 200 g?

5 10 g weights balance 200 g?

6 10 g weights balance 250 g?

C Answer these without using scales. How many:

☆ 5 g weights balance 50 g?   10

1 5 g weights balance 20 g?

2 20 g weights balance 100 g?

3 5 g weights balance 100 g?

4 20 g weights balance 200 g?

5 20 g weights balance 120 g?

6 5 g weights balance 55 g?

B Is the total weight in each group heavier or lighter than $\frac{1}{2}$ kg?

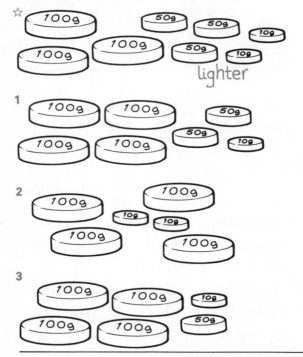

D Write weights that will balance each object:

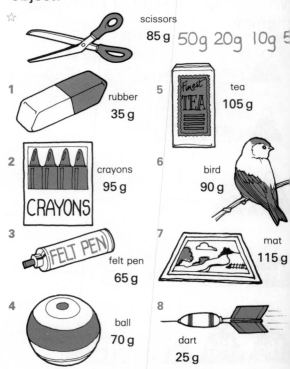

☆ scissors 85 g   50g 20g 10g 5

1 rubber 35 g

2 crayons 95 g

3 felt pen 65 g

4 ball 70 g

5 tea 105 g

6 bird 90 g

7 mat 115 g

8 dart 25 g

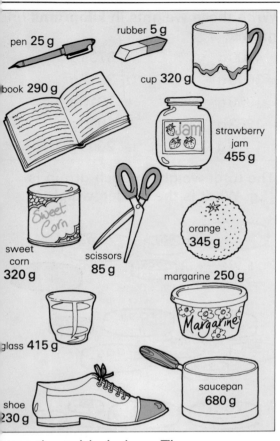

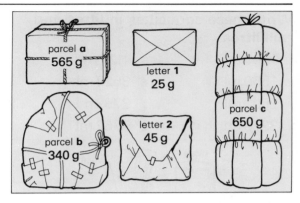

Copy the table below. Then, complete the table by writing weights to balance each object:

objects	weights					
	500 g	100 g	50 g	20 g	10 g	5 g
pen					|	|
rubber						
cup						
book						
jam						
sweetcorn						
scissors						
shoe						
orange						
glass						
saucepan						
margarine						

B Work out the total weight of:

☆ parcel **a** and parcel **b**
$$\begin{array}{r} 565g \\ +340g \\ \hline 905g \end{array}$$

1 parcel **a** and letter **1**

2 parcel **c** and parcel **b**

3 letter **2** and letter **1**

4 parcel **c**, letter **1** and letter **2**

C What is the difference in weight between:

☆ parcel **b** and parcel **c**?
$$\begin{array}{r} 650g \\ -340g \\ \hline 310g \end{array}$$

1 parcel **a** and parcel **b**?

2 letter **1** and letter **2**?

3 letter **2** and parcel **c**?

4 parcel **a** and parcel **c**?

D Use division to answer these:

☆ 3 egg cups each have the same weight. Together they weigh 96 g. What is the weight of 1 egg-cup?
$$\begin{array}{r} 32g \\ 3\overline{)96g} \end{array}$$

1 8 pencils each have the same weight. Together they weigh 96 g. What is the weight of 1 pencil?

2 4 rulers each have the same weight. Together they weigh 72 g. What is the weight of 1 ruler?

3 7 cards each have the same weight. Together they weigh 84 g. What is the weight of 1 card?

A Write these capacities in **litres** and **millilitres**:

1	1200 ml	5	4127 ml
2	1550 ml	6	3628 ml
3	2500 ml	7	2793 ml
4	3275 ml	8	7762 ml

B

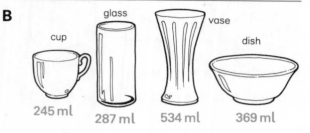

cup · glass · vase · dish

245 ml   287 ml   534 ml   369 ml

1 Work out the total capacity of the glass and the dish.
2 What is the difference in capacity between the vase and the cup?
3 How much water would be required to fill the glass 3 times?
4 What is the total capacity of the glass, the cup and the dish?

C How many cubes in each cuboid?

1

4

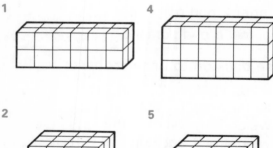

2

5

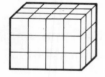

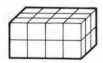

3

6

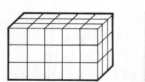

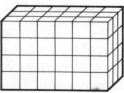

D Write these weights in **kilograms** and **grams**:

1	4200 g	6	5705 g
2	3600 g	7	3337 g
3	1950 g	8	2016 g
4	1263 g	9	5050 g
5	1476 g	10	2005 g

E The total weight in each group is $\frac{1}{2}$ **kg**. What is the hidden weight?

1

2

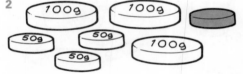

3

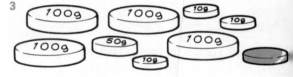

4

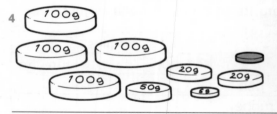

F Write weights that will balance each object:

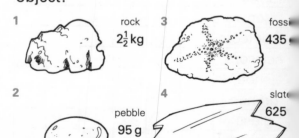

1   rock $2\frac{1}{2}$ kg

3   fossi   435

2   pebble   95 g

4   slate   625

We can use multiplication to find how many cubes in this layer.
There are **6** cubes along and **2** cubes across.

$$6×2=12$$

There are **12** cubes in the layer.

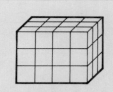

We can use multiplication to find how many cubes in this cuboid.

There are **12** cubes in each layer.
There are **3** layers.
There are **36** cubes in the cuboid.

$$\begin{array}{r} 12 \\ \times 3 \\ \hline 36 \end{array}$$

Use multiplication to find how many cubes in each of these layers:

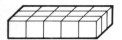

$5×3=15$

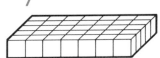

6

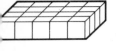

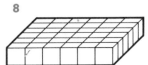

7

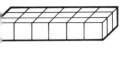

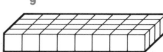

8

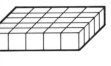

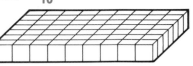

9

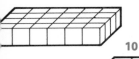

10

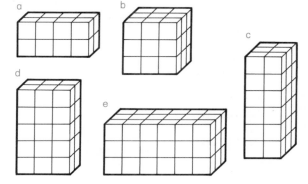

B Copy and complete:

	cuboid	number of cubes in each layer	number of layers	number of cubes in cuboid
☆	a	8	2	16
1	b			
2	c			
3	d			
4	e			

C How many cubes in these cuboids?

☆

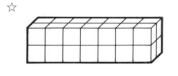

28

1

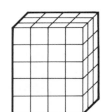

2

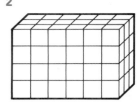

Mixed problems

Work out the answers to these problems:

In a school there are 186 boys and 209 girls. How many children are there altogether?   395

Farmer Brown has 385 sheep and Farmer Bloggs has 268 sheep. How many more sheep has Farmer Brown than Farmer Bloggs?

Cakes cost 15p each. What is the cost of 6 cakes?

In 3 throws at darts, Ann scores 27, 68 and 92. How many does she score altogether?

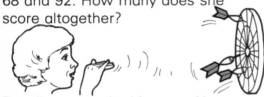

Pencils are packed in tens. How many packs can be filled with 100 pencils?

There are 124 boxes in a crate. How many boxes in 4 crates?

Mrs Toms plants 298 flowers on Saturday and 254 flowers on Sunday. How many flowers does she plant altogether on these two days?

Mr Moneybags buys a television set and a video recorder. The television costs £423 and the video costs £438. How much does he spend altogether?

B Find the answers to these problems:

☆ A builder stacks his bricks in piles of 112 bricks. How many bricks in 6 piles?   672

1 If 4 children are each given an equal share of 96 sweets, how many sweets do they each receive?

2 If 268 people are on a train and 109 leave the train at a station, how many people are left on the train?

3 7 pens each have the same weight. Together they weigh 98 grams. What is the weight of 1 pen?

4 There are 24 blocks in each layer of a cuboid. How many blocks are there in 4 layers?

5 What is the difference in length between two ships if one measures 156 metres and the other measures 291 metres?

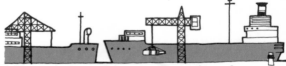

6 If each barrel has a capacity of 31 litres, what is the total capacity of 5 barrels?

Write any 3-figure number

	example		example
	267		583

example 267		example 583
$2 \times 2 = 4$	multiply the first figure by 2	$5 \times 2 = 10$
$4 + 1 = 5$	add 1 to your answer	$10 + 1 = 11$
$5 \times 5 = 25$	multiply this answer by 5	$11 \times 5 = 55$
$25 + 6 = 31$	add your second figure	$55 + 8 = 63$

$$\begin{array}{r} 3\,1 \\ \times\ \ 2 \\ \hline 6\,2 \end{array} \qquad \text{multiply your answer by 2} \qquad \begin{array}{r} 6\,3 \\ \times\ \ 2 \\ \hline 1\,2\,6 \end{array}$$

$62 + 1 = 63$	add 1 to your answer	$126 + 1 = 127$

$$\begin{array}{r} 6\,3 \\ \times\ \ 5 \\ \hline 3\,1\,5 \end{array} \qquad \text{multiply this answer by 5} \qquad \begin{array}{r} 1\,2\,7 \\ \times\ \ 5 \\ \hline 6\,3\,5 \end{array}$$

$$\begin{array}{r} 3\,1\,5 \\ +\ \ \ 7 \\ \hline 3\,2\,2 \end{array} \qquad \text{add your third figure} \qquad \begin{array}{r} 6\,3\,5 \\ +\ \ \ 3 \\ \hline 6\,3\,8 \end{array}$$

$$\begin{array}{r} 3\,2\,2 \\ -\ \ 5\,5 \\ \hline 2\,6\,7 \end{array} \qquad \text{subtract 55 from your answer} \qquad \begin{array}{r} 6\,3\,8 \\ -\ \ 5\,5 \\ \hline 5\,8\,3 \end{array}$$

267	These are the numbers that were written at the top of the page!	583

A Does this work for these numbers?

1 327 2 483 3 617 4 591 5 602 6 180

B Write down a 3-figure number of your own.
Follow the steps above. Do you come back to your number?